4X 9/09 ✓ 11/09
4X 9/09 ✓ 6/11

Ways of Telling

Also by Leonard S. Marcus

Side by Side: Five Favorite Picture-Book Teams Go to Work

Author Talk

Dear Genius: The Letters of Ursula Nordstrom

A Caldecott Celebration: Six Artists and the Paths to the Caldecott Medal

The Making of Goodnight Moon: *A 50th Anniversary Retrospective*

75 Years of Children's Book Week Posters

Lifelines: A Poetry Anthology Patterned on the Stages of Life

Margaret Wise Brown: Awakened by the Moon

WAYS OF TELLING

Conversations
on the
ART
of the
Picture Book

Leonard S. Marcus

Dutton Children's Books • New York

For Donna Brooks

CIP Data is available.

Published in the United States by Dutton Children's Books,
a division of Penguin Putnam Books for Young Readers
345 Hudson Street, New York, New York 10014
www.penguinputnam.com

Designed by Sara Reynolds
Printed in USA
First Edition
ISBN 0-525-46490-5
1 3 5 7 9 10 8 6 4 2

Acknowledgments

Some of these interviews were previously published, in somewhat abbreviated form, as follows: Mitsumasa Anno, Robert McCloskey, Helen Oxenbury, and Maurice Sendak, in *Parenting* magazine; Iona Opie, in *The Lion and the Unicorn*. My interview with the late James Marshall was recorded as background for a profile first published in *Publishers Weekly*.

I wish to thank each of the writers and illustrators who participated in these interviews. I am grateful to them for the time they gave and for their willingness to speak freely about their lives and work.

I wish also to thank Deanne Urmy for her early interest in this project and Donna Brooks and the staff of Dutton Children's Books for their help in seeing it through to completion.

Contents

Ways of Telling

Introduction

This is a portrait, in interview form, of fourteen artists and writers who have made extraordinary contributions to the art of the picture book and the culture of childhood.

A picture book is a dialogue between two worlds: the world of images and the world of words. This is a book of conversations about that beguiling dialogue.

Picture books also forge a dialogue between generations: between the artists and writers who create them and the children who compose their primary audience. To connect with that audience, picture book makers must distill their ideas down to what mathematicians call "simplest terms"—to their clearest possible form.

Loneliness, love, the longing for adventure are familiar themes of drama, literature, painting—and the picture book. But in the case of an art form so deliberately rooted in artless appearances, older readers may be forgiven their sense of surprise when a book aimed at the comprehension of four-year-olds turns out also to hold interest for themselves. In the pages that follow, that sense of surprise at picture books will not, I trust, be in any way diminished. But I hope that it will be re-directed toward a fuller, better appreciation of the hidden artistry at work in the picture books we remember. A four-year-old can live in a house, but it takes an architect to build a house. It takes more than an "inner child" to make a picture book that lasts.

What do picture books, with their child-sized blocks of type and few handfuls of images, have to do with literature and art, with the cultural traditions and trends we study in school, read about on the review pages of magazines, see celebrated on public television and at museums? What role do such "simple" books play, not just at story hour but in the life and times of our culture? It has been easy enough to assume nothing. Yet as the interviews in this collection make clear, the legacy of the Great Depression and World War II figure largely in the background and work of several of these artists and writers. The pathfinding discoveries of twentieth-century psychology, which made apparent the developmental value of books for even the youngest children, inform their craft. The Civil Rights and women's rights movements, American Scene painting and Abstract Expressionism, and pop media from comic books to television and film—all have played roles in their education and influenced their creative choices.

The fourteen artists and writers interviewed in this collection have each achieved, over time, a firm, clear vision of the art they practice. They are not, however, offered up as a picture book pantheon. The roster might well have been expanded, and almost any reader is bound to feel the absence of some cherished favorite. In choosing my subjects, I concentrated on the older generations, whose books (or at any rate some of whose books), in this age of instant classics, have already stood the test of time. I have chosen artists and writers, regardless of their country of origin, whose books have had a major impact in the United States. The case of Mitsumasa Anno is particularly noteworthy in this regard. From his studio in Japan, Anno has created picture books that reflect not only Japanese curiosity about Western culture but also the worldly wish for a pictorial storytelling language that children of both cultures might share.

I have included a conversation with the English scholar of child lore, Iona Opie, for several reasons. First, the nursery rhymes and playground chants that she and her late husband commented on served as the texts for some of the first true picture books. Mother Goose rhymes like "Hey, Diddle, Diddle" and "Sing a Song of Sixpence" inspired the nineteenth-century illustrator Randolph Caldecott to explode the static format of the traditional illustrated book and offer in its place the kinetic, mixed-media art form that we now honor with the medal bearing his name. The Opies, moreover, have contributed as much as anyone in our time to our understanding of the communal culture of children of the picture book ages. And finally, as though by a Mother Goose–rendering of poetic justice, a growing portion of the Opies' scholarly gleanings have been turned back in recent years, by Iona Opie herself, for the delight of new generations of children, in books illustrated by Maurice Sendak, Rosemary Wells, and others.

In each of these interviews, I have searched for the thread or threads that connect the life work to the life story and individual works to one another. How have these artists and writers grown? Who were their mentors? What impelled these gifted men and women to devote their adult lives to the literature of childhood? For the majority of them, the cultural climate was hardly favorable. Until quite recently, few museums considered the art for such books worthy of exhibition; few art schools offered much in the way of professional training or encouragement. And picture book writers, on the whole, may be said to have fared even less well than artists in terms of respect and recognition from their peers. When as young independent scholars in the 1940s Iona and Peter Opie began their study of the lore of the nursery, they, too, encountered the scorn and skepticism of literary lions proud themselves of having put away "childish things" forever.

Artists and writers need not know why they work as they do—why, for instance, they prefer pen-and-ink to watercolor, or why certain themes rather than others engage their imagination. But some artists and writers do know the answers or can begin, at any rate, to say what their answers to such questions might possibly be. Several of those interviewed here have worked as teachers and so have had practical experience at formulating answers to satisfy the curiosity of others. All fourteen are storytellers and know that the best answer to some questions is not an answer but a tale. In the conversations that follow, they tell the stories behind some of the best-loved children's books of the last half century.

Mitsumasa Anno

Born March 20, 1926
Tsuwano, Japan

....

W hen I was a child," Mitsumasa Anno once recalled, "I pictured the world-is-round concept as a rubber ball turned inside out with the people of the different continents living inside the ball. Of course, it was a boy's way of imagining. . . . But this kind of imagination . . . is another sort of eye for perceiving what things really are. And it is the source of all [my] books."

A robust, barrel-chested man with an intense but mischievous manner, Anno came of age artistically in the 1970s, at a time when idealistic editors in the United States, Europe, and Japan were eager to publish picture books cooperatively. Hoping to foster a spirit of international understanding among children, the editors also saw an opportunity in such joint ventures to hold down the cost of color printing through the economies of scales to be gained from larger than ordinary print runs. In order to succeed, the picture books they championed naturally had to have broad appeal. Mitsumasa Anno, with his brilliant knack for visual storytelling, his traveler's knowledge of the world, and deep curiosity about cultural similarities and differences, proved the perfect artist to meet the challenge.

Anno's first picture book, Topsy-Turvies: Pictures to Stretch the Imagination, was published in 1970. Anno's Alphabet (1975), Anno's

Journey (1977), Anno's Medieval World (1980), and Anno's Mysterious Multiplying Jar (1983) are among the subsequent works that steadily added to his reputation as an innovator and latter-day Renaissance man. In 1984, Anno received children's literature's highest honor, the international Hans Christian Andersen Medal, in recognition of his "unique [gift for] communicating to both East and West."

In Japan, where nearly all youngsters grow up knowing his picture books, Anno is also celebrated for his books for adult readers on mathematics, philosophy, history, and travel, for his striking magazine-cover designs, and his lively television talks on art and history. In March 2001, he took part in the opening ceremonies of the Mitsumasa Anno Museum, a showcase for his lifetime of art making, located in his hometown, Tsuwano, Japan.

This interview was recorded at the Hotel Kitano in New York, on April 22, 1989, with Akiko Kurita serving as interpreter.

Leonard S. Marcus: Adults sometimes assume that young children don't think abstractly. Judging from your books, you don't agree.

Mitsumasa Anno: A young child might not understand Picasso, but if I draw a circle and add a short line at the top for a stem, even a two-year-old will see that it's an apple. No color is needed, just the outline. This is one of a child's first steps toward abstract understanding. And if I make a simple drawing with circles for heads and rectangles for bodies and single lines for arms and legs, a child will understand me when I say, "This is Father. This is Mother." Adults take such leaps for granted. That a two-year-old can do so is a kind of miracle.

LSM: Your books seem aimed at challenging preconceived ideas about the world and encouraging independent thinking. Anno's Medieval World, for instance, concerns the difficulty that people once had in accepting the notion that the world was round.

MA: A child's mind, unlike an adult's, can absorb anything and accept any number of new ideas. For this reason, it is not always good to teach only "correct" ideas to children. Scientific understanding is important, but imagination should also be encouraged. When some adults see a rainbow, they think they must explain the color spectrum to a child. The sense of wonder at such things should come first.

Recently, I spoke to a group of schoolchildren in Sydney, Australia. I told them that I had been afraid to come "down under" to Sydney lest I fall off the earth on my way. They laughed and then explained to me that "the world is round but there are also some flat places where it is safe." These children did not yet know the difference between imagination and reality. It is important to let them imagine things in their own way for a while before teaching them differently.

LSM: Your first book to become well known in the United States was *Anno's Alphabet*. Why did you make a book about the Roman alphabet—the alphabet of Western languages?

MA: One day when I was tired I found myself looking at the corner of a table. Just then two converging sides of the tabletop and the leg below began to look to me like a letter *T*. I made a drawing of what I had seen and began to wonder whether Westerners, who were used to thinking of a *T* as a flat, printed symbol, would realize that my drawing of the table corner and leg was also a *T*. The book evolved from there.

LSM: In your *Alphabet*, as well as in *Topsy-Turvies*, you seem fascinated by visual paradoxes and illusions.

MA: In 1960 or 1961, after having taught school for ten years, I went to Paris. I did not as yet have any intention of making children's books. I wanted to paint. It was during that time that I first saw the illusionist prints and drawings of the Dutch graphic

9 •

artist M. C. Escher. Escher's work greatly excited me. Unlike some modern art, his style is easily understood. I began to think that his images might please children as much as they pleased me, and I realized that no one had done an alphabet using that technique before. At first I thought the letters would make a good picture book by themselves, but my Japanese publisher asked me to add companion pictures for each letter.

LSM: *Anno's Alphabet* doesn't simply begin with the letter A, as do most alphabet books. You first show a question mark carved out of wood, then a tree . . . and finally, a carving in the form of a book— an alphabet book. That initial sequence of pages reminds me of the opening credits of a film.

MA: That is exactly what I wanted. I think of all my books as films.

LSM: *Anno's Alphabet* was published both in Japan and in the West. Did creating a book for such a diverse audience influence your choice of imagery?

MA: Very definitely. I drew an angel, for example, to illustrate the letter A. It looked rather like a baby with swan's wings. But when the American and British editors saw my drawing, they said, "This is not an angel! It's a cupid." I replied that it looked like an angel to me. My drawing, you see, was similar to the angel trademark of a well-known Japanese confectioner. The incident underscored for me the fact that pictorial images do not necessarily carry the same associations from culture to culture. I had to give up my angel and replace it with a picture of an anvil.

Then, in the decorative border for the letter B, I drew a type of bean that I thought would surely be recognizable to everyone in the West. I had checked it in an encyclopedia! I knew we had the same type of bean in Japan, so I proceeded to do my drawing. Nevertheless, my American editor objected, "That bean is too short. Make it longer!" Whereupon, I produced my encyclopedia. My editor would still have none of it. "We don't see our beans in books," she said. "We see them in the supermarket." So I had to redraw the entire rather complicated border. Later I found that my book showed an older type of bean that was no longer widely available. Many such changes were necessary.

LSM: The border drawings in your *Alphabet* contain small details that a young child might not notice but that might very well intrigue the same child years later. Do you intentionally create drawings with different layers that, in a sense, run parallel to children's education and development?

MA: In one of the scenes in *Anno's Journey*, I incorporated a rendering of *The Gleaners*, a well-known work by the nineteenth-century French painter Jean-François Millet, in which peasant women are seen at work in a field. When a small child sees those women in the book, he doesn't know the source of that particular image but can make up his own story about them—who they are, what they are thinking about, in what kind of house each one lives, and so on. Later he may see the Millet painting and remember the women.

As a child, I would do much the same thing. I liked to observe people and make up stories about them. If a man walked by, I would decide that he must be a carpenter, or a doctor on his way to see a child in the hospital, or whatever.

LSM: In the *Journey* books you have mixed together imaginary scenes with images from the real world—for instance, in *Anno's U.S.A.* (1983), a scene from *Shane* and landmarks such as the Empire State Building and Independence Hall. What do you want children to learn from this?

MA: That imagination, which is about impossibility, and reality aren't opposites, but complement each other. One might say that reality and imagination differ from each other in the same way that the audience at a play is set apart from the actors. It's where the two meet that hope is to be found.

In my books, I don't want to teach. What I have done might better be described as "teaching without teaching"—providing the conditions that allow children to learn for themselves. I once heard about a little boy who excitedly showed the Superman picture in *Anno's U.S.A.* to his teacher. She acted surprised, even though she knew it was there. This teacher's response allowed the child to feel the joy of having made a personal discovery.

LSM: In format, the *Journey* books resemble traditional Japanese picture scrolls, yet the countries depicted in your stories—Britain, Italy, the U.S.A.—are all Western.

MA: When I made *Anno's Journey*, I did not intend to use the traditional picture-scroll form. It simply came out that way. What I had set out to do was to draw pictures from a certain distance—in terms of time as well as of space. You will find many historical details in my pictures. The reader's perspective on time is expanded as a result. The *Journey* books also show different portions of the world's geography, expanding the reader's sense of space, too.

LSM: Why haven't you made a *Journey* book about your native Japan?

MA: The essence of being human is the same everywhere. Many Westerners have told me, "You know more about Europe and the United States than we do." But everywhere in the world, if there is a road and a river, there is always a bridge. In making my books, I have been seeking archetypes that transcend any particular culture. I have looked for images that people everywhere would know.

LSM: Have you also made some books on specifically Japanese themes?

MA: At the moment, I am working on a historical picture book for older children and adults, *The Tale of the Heike*. It is a classic

Japanese war story that was first written down in the thirteenth century. It tells of the powerful Heike clan, who enjoyed prosperity for a time but was then defeated in battle by the rival Genji clan and faded away into the western sea. The story is a beautiful description of human destiny.

LSM: Would you tell me something about the place where you were born?

MA: I was born in Tsuwano, a village surrounded by mountains in the west of Japan, on the "sea side" as we say. Now it has become a tourist town and is called "Little Kyoto." But when I was a boy, an airplane would fly over our village maybe once a year. We would catch a brief glimpse of it between the mountains. That, for us, was very exciting.

Because of all the mountains, we could not see the ocean, which to me as a small boy seemed very far away. I couldn't believe that seawater was salty. I was ten years old when I first saw the ocean for myself, and when no one was looking I reached down to taste the water.

My parents kept an inn, where I helped out as a child. From that experience, I determined that I would never keep an inn myself!

LSM: Did you like to draw as a child?

MA: Yes, I began on my own as a small boy, drawing mountains, houses, and ghosts.

LSM: How did you know what a ghost looked like?

MA: Years later, when I was doing the illustrations for *Anno's Alphabet*, I drew a devil to illustrate the letter *D*. My British editor looked at it and said, "That's not a devil!" And so I asked this person, "Have you seen a devil yourself?" She replied that she had not, but that in her own mind she was sure how a devil would look. She proceeded to make all kinds of gestures in order to show me her idea of a devil. From that exchange I realized that there are many invisible things that have never actually existed but which, nonetheless, exist in people's minds as quite specific images.

LSM: What pictures and images influenced you as a young artist?

MA: It was thanks to my parents' inn that as a child I saw all kinds of magazines that were left around for the guests. Looking through those magazines, I was exposed to all sorts of pictures, from classical to modern in style. Even as a child I thought that an artist should be free to work in any number of styles to suit his purposes. Now I have my own style, but I still think it is important for an artist to feel that freedom.

LSM: Did the art teachers you went on to study with feel the same way?

MA: Not at all. But then later, when I myself taught drawing and painting to children, I realized that, aside from technique, drawing and painting cannot be taught. Most people think that the technique is the art. That is a great misunderstanding.

LSM: Were there books you especially liked as a child?

MA: Lots of books. I had no picture books, though—only the magazines. I read Mark Twain in Japanese.

LSM: Did you find that teaching children was more or less what you expected it would be like?

MA: School did not totally prepare me for what lay ahead, but in any case I wanted to experiment in my teaching. On the first day of class, the cherry blossoms were all out, and I asked each child to bring a flower into the classroom. When I was a child of eleven, my teacher had shown me how to draw this flower. So now I sketched the same drawing on the blackboard for my students. I showed them the stamens and pistils—the male and female parts of the flower. I explained that everything in nature is made up of male and female parts. In my drawing—my teacher hadn't done this—I added a bee heading straight for the flower.

In the classroom there was also a camellia, which has a great many petals. The children said, "This camellia has no pistils!" To which I replied, "No, you are not correct." Then in order to prove it, I opened all the petals—and found no pistils, just stamens.

LSM: At least you taught them well. They had really looked.

MA: Yes, but I was vexed because what I said had not been true!

LSM: That's often the case with teachers. [laughter]

MA: Later when I was visiting a museum in Tokyo, I asked someone why this was so and was told that the pistils become the camellia's petals. That's why camellias have so many.

LSM: What else did you do to engage their interest?

MA: One day I had planned to take the children outdoors to draw in the wheat fields. I was thinking of a particular painting by van Gogh with crows flying over a wheat field and wondered how the children would draw such a scene. Suddenly, however, it began to pour, and so the children had to stay indoors. Abandoning our original plan, I went outdoors myself and picked a single stalk of wheat from the field and brought it back to the classroom, where I drew a picture of it on the blackboard. I explained that the wheat field was really just a collection of stalks like the one I had brought in, and that they could draw the whole field by seeing only a single stalk. And so they did.

The next day I had another group of children. This time the weather was fine, so we went outdoors to sketch in the fields. When you look at such a field, it's like looking at a toothbrush. You can't see each individual bristle or stalk, and so you can't draw it effectively that way, either. But that is exactly what those children tried to do—with so many upright strokes that their pictures were all black! Their pictures didn't look at all like the field. The children who stayed indoors produced pictures that were more abstract, that picked out only the important details. Ironically, the children who stayed indoors were the ones who could draw the real field.

LSM: The drawings in your books are beautiful, as well as imaginative. What role does beauty play in children's books?

MA: All beautiful things encourage a child's sense of wonder—and everything that encourages a child's sense of wonder is beautiful. In my three *Math Games* books and several others, I have tried to show that mathematics is beautiful and not necessarily difficult—that math is primarily a way of thinking about things.

LSM: One of the unusual aspects of *Anno's Counting Book* is that you start not with the number one, as is typical, but with zero. Did you have a hard time deciding how to express the concept of zero pictorially?

MA: Zero is not simply "nothing" but "something missing." A mentally retarded boy was once looking at the book. He started at the end, where the number twelve is illustrated in a scene with twelve houses, twelve trees, twelve reindeer, and so on. "Oh, there are so many houses," he said. Then as he turned the pages and there were fewer and fewer of everything, he said, "Getting lonely." When he turned from the picture for the number three, with three houses, to the picture for two, he said, "House disappeared." Finally, when the boy came to the picture for zero, which is just a snowy field through which a river is running, he sighed and said, "Now we have nothing." I was very moved by this child.

LSM: In your *Math Games* you present a series of mathematical ideas, starting with simple ones and progressing to more challenging concepts. Are these books to be read through all at once?

MA: There may well be some concepts that a younger child will not be ready to understand, and in that case the parent should skip those pages and wait until the child is ready. But as I show in those books, there are many real-life illustrations of mathematical ideas in a child's own world, and all one has to do is point them out to the child and he will understand—without having to be taught.

LSM: So the world itself can be viewed as a kind of picture book, as a series of illustrations from which a child will learn?

MA: Yes. For instance, if you have two brothers at home, and one of them is a "bigger quantity" and the other is a "smaller quantity," a child immediately knows the difference. That is mathematics. Children can, of course, be taught such things in the traditional manner. But a child's joy is always much greater when he makes the discovery for himself.

················

Ashley Bryan

Born July 13, 1923
The Bronx, New York

....

A s an illustrator, painter, printmaker,
writer, folklorist, and storyteller, Ashley
Bryan has created a vibrant and amazingly var-
ied body of work both for children and adults.
Bryan's African-American heritage has inspired
much of this remarkable output, including the
lion's share of the more than thirty children's
books he has written and/or illustrated since the
late 1960s. Throughout his career, however,
Bryan has also remained receptive to a wide
range of other creative influences, including Japanese brush painting, the
study of philosophy, medieval wood-block art, Mother Goose nonsense,
and the thoughtful comments of his school-age Maine friends. Time and
again, he has borne out the truth of the Tuscan proverb that "the story is
not beautiful unless something is added to it." Something, that is, of the
storyteller's own most deeply felt experience.

Perhaps no other living artist can claim both to have taught painting
to kindergartners and to have chaired the art department of a major
American institution of higher learning—Dartmouth College. To Bryan,
however, there is nothing incongruous about this broad span of activity.
A tall, articulate man with a warm and ready laugh, he approaches every
aspect of his work as a learning experience and has, therefore, always felt

a genuine sense of comradeship with his students, whatever their age. Although Bryan no longer teaches, he spends half of each year on the road, giving poetry readings and storytelling performances for school-children and other audiences throughout the world.

Bryan spoke with me by telephone from his studio in Maine on October 30, 1999.

LEONARD S. MARCUS: How did you get started making books?

ASHLEY BRYAN: In the public school I attended in the South Bronx during the Great Depression years, we began early on making books about whatever we learned. As we learned the alphabet, for instance, we did pictures for the letters and then sewed them together, and our teacher would say, "You've just published an alphabet book!" That was the beginning. There was a lot of fun and play associated with our bookmaking. Our teacher would say, "You're the author, you're the illustrator, you're the publisher. Take it home. You're the distributor!" I got such a warm response at home from my parents and brothers and sisters and the cousins who were growing up with us that I just kept making books as gifts. I never stopped, and it was that initial satisfaction that sustained me later, when there was no commercial interest in my work. It took over fifteen years before my work was finally picked up on.

LSM: Despite the depression, you seem to have had a wonderful introduction to art and learning.

AB: Thanks to the WPA, there were free art and music classes in the community where we lived and throughout the country. My parents sent us children out to whatever was free. They said, "Learn to entertain yourselves." That idea was behind it all. So my brothers, my sisters, and I were all painting, drawing, and playing instruments. The WPA teachers were very exciting for me as a nine-, ten-, and eleven-year-old. I might paint an apple red or green, for instance, and then the instructor would show us works of the Impressionists and explain how a fruit could be explored in many different colors, while still giving the impression of its color. I was fascinated and would play around with these ideas.

LSM: What was it like growing up in the Bronx during those years?

AB: Our neighborhood and my public school were ethnically and racially quite mixed, with German, Irish, Italian, Jewish, and black people living on the same streets. There was a fairly tolerant atmosphere. Next to our school was a German Lutheran church, and it was so big and so pretty that we children said to our parents, "We want to go to that great big pretty church." So my mother did take us. Services were both in German and in English. And we grew up in that church, which was always active in the community.

LSM: Did you go to the public library in your neighborhood?

AB: Oh, yes. Although we children could not afford to buy books, we borrowed books from the library and felt that they were our books for the time that we had them out. We used to clip coupons from the daily newspaper, and at a certain point, when you had enough coupons, you could trade them in for a book. It meant so much to me to have a book of my own. I can remember seeing listed among the books to send in for *The Sketch Book,* by Washington Irving, and thinking it was a book of drawings. So I did send in for it and was surprised to find a drawing only on the title page. At home we had orange crates on which to set our books. That was our library.

LSM: Were certain books special to you then?

AB: Oh, yes. Basically, it was poetry and folktales and fairy tales, which I read quite exhaustively. Poetry, from Mother Goose to Robert Louis Stevenson's *A Child's Garden of Verses* to Eugene Field's *Poems of Childhood* to Christina Rossetti's *Sing-Song: A Nurs-*

ery Rhyme Book. I loved poetry, and I began to explore poetry myself. I didn't take to novels until later, because I didn't go for the long reading of a book. I loved stories that could be told within a brief span of pages. I relished the language and would go back over words that seemed nicely placed. I would read a paragraph that thrilled me with a sense of adventure or the beauty of words, and would stop, go back, and read it again.

LSM: Were you a good student?

AB: I was a very good student academically all the way through. I was in high school, wondering whether I would be a doctor or lawyer or whatever, when I decided that, having always drawn and painted, I wanted to study art. And so during my senior year, I put together a portfolio with the help of my teachers, all of whom were white and were very supportive of me.

LSM: Did your parents encourage you, too?

AB: I was very fortunate in that it never occurred to them that I would not go on doing what I loved to do. The point my parents always made was that if you are doing something creative and constructive, there is no reason not to continue. And so, as a teacher, I found a way to keep doing what I enjoyed while also continuing to make art. Now when I speak to schoolchildren, I tell them, "You need encouragement. If you can't get it at home, knock on the door next door and keep on knocking all the way down until you come to someone who will encourage you in the constructive, creative work that you are doing."

LSM: Tell me about your grandmother, the one who spent time with your family when you were growing up.

AB: She was such a wonderful person. Granny Sarah Bryan was my father's mother. Both my parents had left Antigua at the end of World War I and settled in New York City. My grandmother had not seen my father, or all but one of her other children, in many

Ashley Bryan

21 •

years when she came to visit us in the Bronx. I just loved being with her and got to talking with her, asking her questions. I would sit with her, drawing all the time. I can even remember once drawing her when it was evening, and she was in her nightgown sitting on her bed. I was sitting in a nearby chair when a friend walked in and my grandmother, who was very quick, looked up and said, "Ee oh me hus-bend"—"He is my husband." She was so witty, and she loved to dance. My book *The Dancing Granny* (1977) is an African tale collected in Antigua, and it has as one of its two main characters spider Anansi, the trickster. I did that book to bring out the spirit of the dance that my grandmother had in her. She would outdance the great-grandchildren. She used to say, "The music sweet me so!" I used that phrase in retelling the story. In the original, spider continually gets away with his tricks. That, of course, is generally the point of trickster tales—that the trickster gets away with mischief. But when I was basing my story on the motif, I thought, well, he might trick my grandma a few times, but she's eventually going to figure out what he's up to, and she's going to get him! So that is why in my version, I worked it to the point where she waits for him and catches him before he can get up into that tree, and then they have to dance together, and "As the lead bends/The dance goes on, but the story ends."

LSM: Is that your grandmother pictured in the drawings of *The Dancing Granny?*

AB: Well, it's her spirit. Children ask: "Could your granny really do that?" And I say, "Listen, my friends, if you don't exaggerate, a story won't come true to life." I used swift brush paintings in the spirit of the Japanese brush-painter Hokusai, in his scenes of everyday life, to capture the swift spirit of the moving figure. When I look at those pictures I can still see my granny alive and spinning. She was about ninety-four when she died.

LSM: You served in the army during World War II. Would you tell me about your experiences during those years?

AB: I was in my third year in the Cooper Union Art School when I was drafted. It was a time of segregated armies, and most blacks were in the transportation corps. I was assigned to a stevedore battalion responsible for loading and unloading cargo at docks. I was first stationed in Boston, then sent to Scotland, where we were stationed in Glasgow. Then we went in as part of the Normandy invasion. The beaches were heavily mined, many lives were lost, and I was fortunate in having survived that experience.

LSM: It must have been emotionally complicated to be fighting for freedom in a segregated army.

AB: It was very difficult when you were finally in it, because you went in with ideals but were quickly weighed down by what you were experiencing. We were continually facing restrictions both in Boston and Glasgow because the army did not want the black soldiers to go out and meet with the white population.

LSM: Were you able to continue to draw during those years?

AB: I always had drawing materials with me, which I stuffed into my gas mask. Whenever I had an opportunity, I would take out my drawing materials and sketch whatever was going on. In Glasgow, I went to the battalion commander and got permission to attend the Glasgow School of Art. The other fellows, who were faced with the usual restrictions, always supported me when I went off to class, because they thought I was putting something over on the officers. I thought I was fighting for my right to keep growing as an artist.

When I returned to Cooper Union to complete my studies, I had an exhibition of the drawings and paintings I had done during the war. But because of the experiences of the army and the war, I found I could not go on directly in art. So instead I did my undergraduate work all over again, as a philosophy major at Columbia

Ashley Bryan

University. I was trying to get some understanding of why it is that we continually choose war. Of course there were no answers, but I became very caught up in the way the mind works, how man constructs philosophical systems of ethics and politics and aesthetics. Summers, I would come up to Maine, to the Cranberry Isles, which I had discovered while at Cooper Union. I was awarded a scholarship to The Skowhegan School of Painting and Sculpture in Maine, in the year of its founding, 1946. I would paint through the summer, and when I returned to my studies in New York I would always keep a sketchbook at hand. Sketchbooks for me are always the connection to the mystery and wonder of marking a blank space and seeing something emerge from it. And so I would draw but was not able to go more deeply into the work. But as soon as I completed my work at Columbia, I went to Aix-en-Provence, in the south of France, where, under the G.I. Bill, I began to paint all day.

LSM: Did your interest in philosophy merge with your early interest in folklore? Characters in folk stories so often represent basic types—the trickster, the fool—that add up to a kind of philosophy of human potential.

AB: The mind tends to make connections, and I have always felt that whatever I learn becomes integrated with everything else. And yes, I came to feel that the stories of the world tend to bring us together. I speak of folk stories as a "tender bridge," as a way of connecting past cultures and times to the present.

LSM: When did you begin telling stories before a live audience?

AB: It was a natural extension of my work as a teacher. I have always been teaching—at universities, in after-school programs for elementary school children. At the Dalton School in New York, I taught drawing and painting to kindergartners and first graders. All of my work as a teacher has involved story. The most important aspect of story is the way one person speaks to another. Children pick up on story simply from all the things that other people say to them, the answers their parents give, for example, to their questions. "What was it like when you were growing up?" "Would you tell me that story again about when you were on the boat coming over from your country to this country?" All of this is oral tradition to the child. It becomes a part of their lives. If they become writers, they will draw upon those sources. If they don't, they will still pass those stories along, with their own additions to them. In that sense, story is always going on. When I'm teaching a class in painting and drawing, there's a kind of storytelling that plays an active part in it as well. I'm not talking now about the literal sense of working from a story in a book, of interpreting visually a tale about a king or a queen or a princess. It is also a kind of storytelling when a student, coming to terms with an exercise, finds an inventive way, for instance, of relating a series of straight lines marked across a page to the trunks of trees.

LSM: What did you like best about teaching?

AB: When I taught college students, I loved in particular to work in the introductory courses, teaching basics. Students who had not been drawing or painting for years would begin to make discoveries through the exercises offered. So, for instance, if we worked with straight lines—with divisions between one straight line and another, with questions of spacing and rhythm—we would then go outdoors and draw the trunks of trees. Our goal would be to relate the reality of the trees to the abstraction of lines on a page. I have always tried to connect up with the essentially abstract nature of any art, whether it be dance or painting or poetry.

I would always give my college students set exercises and set limits. I would say, "This is an 8" x 10" paper. This is a pencil. The exercise is to draw these apples on the table. They're your challenge.

When you understand their limits and work with all that you are, then you will be able to surpass those limits." I would tell them, "A Rembrandt drawing was done on a piece of paper of a certain size and shape, and it was because Rembrandt gave of himself that he surpassed the limits of that paper, and he was able to create something invaluable with it. That is what we are after."

LSM: How did you approach teaching art to very young children? What did you do with them?

AB: With the young children it was a question of what they did with me! I enjoyed their absorption in what they were doing. They would become so absorbed that it would be as if time no longer mattered. At the Dalton School, where I taught for many years, I would simply have materials ready for the children—brushes, paper, and a muffin tin for each two children with paints, the primary colors plus green, black, and white. I never said, "Today we'll do this or we'll do that." The children would come in and simply get to work. They would have their ideas. They would go on and on with what they were doing. If a child didn't have an idea, I might say, "Maybe there were some horses . . ." or some such thing, and right away the child would say, "Don't tell me, don't tell me. I know what I want to do!" And they'd go right ahead. My goal was to create a situation in which the children would not be dependent on me but would rather come with a tremendous sense of excitement about whatever it was that they had to offer. I remember one child who, day after day, painted columns of starlike forms in different colors. The other children said to him, "You're always painting stars!" And the child kept on painting stars. After a while some of the other children began painting stars, too. But I never said to him, "You've already done that," which is so often what happens to a child. You let the child go to the limit, the exhaustion of possibility, which is what art is about. Any motif is absolutely endless in its possibilities of exploration, and you don't know beforehand how far a child might like to go with an idea.

LSM: Tell me about meeting Jean Karl, the editor with whom you worked at Atheneum for more than thirty years.

AB: Jean, who founded the children's book department at Atheneum, came up to my studio one day in the Bronx. I wasn't sure what she was interested in, so I brought out paintings to show her of my family and other subjects. She went over to the table where I did my book projects, however, and when she saw the things of that kind that I was doing she simply decided to send me a contract to illustrate Richard Lewis's anthology of poems by Rabindranath Tagore, *Moon, For What Do You Wait?* (1967). Then she asked if she could publish some illustrations I had done for African folktales. I had originally done these paintings, which are often mistaken for block prints or silk-screen paints, for a folklore research project for Pantheon Books. Later the project was bought by the Bollingen Foundation, but my illustrations had, in the end, not been used. I had done the paintings in red, yellow, black, and white—the colors of the ancient rock paintings. I painted them so strictly that I almost felt I was carving an African mask or sculpture as I did them. I then wrote my own retellings of the stories, based on the ethnographers' summaries. As I did my own research, I realized that I wanted to do what storytellers have always done, to flesh out the story motifs by bringing into them any connections from my own life that I felt might help make the stories, when printed, approach the spirit of the oral tradition. That has been my challenge in all that I have done. The stories of *The Ox of the Wonderful Horns and Other African Folktales* (1971), for example, follow that pattern. I research the background of the tribe from which the African tale comes. I always acknowledge the source of the story and then set out to make the story my own.

L S M : How, more specifically, have you gone about trying to capture a sense of the spoken word on paper?

A B : I work from poetry. I use the devices of poetry—close rhyme, rhythm, onomatopoeia, alliteration—to slow the reader and make the reader feel that he or she is hearing a storyteller.

L S M : How do you go about deciding on your visual approach to a given book?

A B : The art that I have drawn upon comes from many different sources depending on the text. In the case of my books of spirituals, for instance, starting with *Walk Together Children* (1974), I used block prints in the spirit of medieval European religious block-printed books. I worked from that tradition in order to connect up the spirituals—which a great many people sing but which very few people realize were the creation of black slaves—and the European tradition of religious music and art. I was stirred by the realization that the slaves had created these songs as a way of being free. The slaves were in chains, they suffered, but they had to give forth something rich and beautiful of themselves. There are thousands of these songs, and they are considered our finest contribution to world music. And yet they were completely overlooked in introductory books for children, which is why I began my series.

L S M : As a child, did you meet older people living in your neighborhood who remembered the days of slavery?

A B : No, and I'm not sure to what extent that history would have been a part of my knowing, and of my asking of questions as a child. You see, in our studies, anything about the black world had to come from family or from the community. It wasn't taught at school. What I got to know of any of the black writers and artists or of black history came from a special reach for it. It was when I was in junior high school or in high school, reaching out through my love of poetry, that I first became aware of the poetry of Paul Laurence

Dunbar, Countee Cullen, and others. Today as I travel around, I find that, even though some books are more readily available, a special reach is still needed. Teachers generally still seem unaware of most of the black poets I talk about when I visit schools. They may know of Langston Hughes. My point has always been: They are writing in English; their work is accessible. I illustrated a book of Nikki Giovanni's poems, *The Sun Is So Quiet* (1996), which is firmly in the tradition of the childhood poems of Stevenson and Field. Her poems are so fresh and unaffected, and yet they are not all that well known.

LSM: Tell me more about your interest in the poetry of Paul Laurence Dunbar. You edited a book of his work, *I Greet the Dawn: Poems* (1978).

AB: He was pursued constantly for the poems he wrote in black dialect. Those are the poems for which he became well known, but they represent only a small percentage of his work, the rest of which is in standard English, in the tradition of Keats and Shelley. I compiled my collection in order to help bring that other work, which is so very touching, and so accessible, to young peoples' attention.

LSM: Would you talk about the illustration style you have used in recent years for full-color books such as *Turtle Knows Your Name* (1989) and *The Night Has Ears: African Proverbs* (1999)?

AB: I am a trained artist, but a strong feeling for the untrained artist has always endured in me. So I am a sophisticated artist working, at times, within the folk tradition. Working in that way, there is a sort of lessening of ambition, of wanting to be good. You just know it's going to be—and what is done is going to be right. It's wonderful to lose yourself in that kind of approach.

LSM: Why did you dedicate *Turtle Knows His Name* in part to your editor Jean Karl?

AB: It was her persistence, I suppose, in keeping after me to do my

Ashley Bryan

books, in much the same way that that Grandma keeps after the little child in the story to learn his name. Jean was so wonderful over the years. I doubt that my work would have reached a wider audience than family or friends without her. The book is also dedicated to a little boy who was living on my island here in Maine, where I myself have lived now for over fifty years and seen whole generations grow up. In some ways, the community atmosphere on the island reminds me very much of the neighborhood in which I was raised.

LSM: I've read that you like to paint by day and illustrate by night. Why do you divide your time in that way?

AB: Painting is at the center of what I do. As a painter, I love to work directly from the landscape. In Maine, from spring until late October, I can be outdoors painting in my garden or down by the ocean. My books are a natural outgrowth of my love of painting. You'll find that throughout the history of art, painters have loved working from texts. Much of the art in museums comes from books, whether it is the Bible or mythology or history. Everyone who reads is seeing images. The artist wants to draw them down. So I have always to find my balance between painting and books.

LSM: Have you ever revisited your old South Bronx neighborhood?

AB: On visits to New York, I do. I have family and friends still living there. About ten years ago, there was a fire at St. John's Evangelical Lutheran Church, where I spent so much of my childhood—that beautiful big church we talked about earlier, with the high vaulted ceilings and stained-glass windows from Germany or Italy with their depictions of Bible stories acted out by blondes and brunettes. In that fire, a major window, a resurrection panel over the altar, was destroyed. I have always supported the church from a distance, and after the fire the church contacted me about designing the replacement window. I had been working for years with beach glass that I pick up here, making my own little windows, but had never done a stained-glass window before. I was thrilled to have this opportunity. I designed a black Christ rising from the tomb with the three Marys—each a different shade of black, to indicate the range of colors of black people in the United States—bearing their ointments. And so my window is up there in the church now, glowing along with all the others.

·················

Eric Carle

Born June 25, 1929
Syracuse, New York

....

At first glance, the lemon-yellow sun that shines down benevolently in so many of Eric Carle's picture books might easily be mistaken for an image from a kindergartner's drawing. It is not by chance that this is so. The "childlike" simplicity of Carle's illustrations is a deftly managed fiction aimed, as is every element of his meticulously crafted work, toward the goal of making books that young children accept as their own.

As a promising design student in Germany, Carle was initiated into the leading-edge European tradition of the applied arts which, during the decades before and after World War II, set out to modernize everything man-made, from typefaces to architecture. Seen purely as design, the airy expanses of white space and streamlined layouts of his picture books have more in common with the Concorde than with The Little Engine That Could. Carle, however, also reaches his audience through the life lessons his gentle fables offer up to them. Stories such as his— about the value of work, the importance of friendship, and the everyday miracle of a caterpillar's metamorphosis—have special meaning, Carle believes, for children just making their own life-altering transition from home to school.

Carle is a precise and energetic man whose large studio hums and whirs on one side with the high-tech clatter of computers and on the other with the old-fashioned rustling and scratching sounds that artists working with papers, pens, and brushes have produced for centuries. While book-making remains the primary focus of his activities, Carle has branched out in recent years to experiment with scenic design and other new art forms. By far the most ambitious project to be launched from the studio is the Eric Carle Museum of Picture Book Art, a child-friendly exhibition space, learning center, and archive located on the campus of Hampshire College, in nearby Amherst, Massachusetts.

On July 28, 1994, the day this interview was recorded at the artist's Massachusetts summer home, Carle was busy gathering material for an autobiographical essay later published in The Art of Eric Carle *(1996).*

LEONARD S. MARCUS: You have written that your father liked to draw. What kinds of drawings did he make?

ERIC CARLE: To entertain me as a child, he would do what I'm doing today—tell stories while drawing pictures of trees and animals and sometimes people. He might say of a queen bee, "Oh, she's a little bigger than the others." Then he would draw a number of bees, point to the largest one, and say, "That's the queen."

LSM: Did he ever speak to you about having wanted to become an artist himself?

EC: Yes, he did. His father had not let him.

LSM: Was it after your first-grade teacher told your mother that you had artistic talent that you began to see yourself in that way?

EC: At that age I did not think in those terms. But even before then, I knew that I enjoyed drawing and that it gave me a lot of satisfaction.

I only have vague feelings about that period of my life. Some time

Eric Carle

ago, I gave a talk in Syracuse, and the nephew of my teacher came to hear me. The following day, we visited my old school building— it's now condominiums!

I've written about my memory of the light streaming in through the windows of my classroom, as a sort of first memory of the experience of beauty. Well, during this last visit I realized, for the first time, why the light made such an impression. The school building is set on a knoll. It has no trees or houses around it, and so the light coming in through the windows is strong. You walk up the street with all these houses and trees, and all of a sudden you get to this building which is not surrounded by anything. I am still amazed that a five-year-old could have had so vivid a response to such an experience.

LSM: What else do you remember about your first year of school?

EC: I still remember the walk there, and the brushes and the papers and the paints and the large colorful paintings I did. I know I had a woman for a teacher, but I don't recall what she looked like, whether she was young or old. Yet to this day I sense her influence and her being, somehow.

From that time onward, I always knew that I would be an artist. I wouldn't have said "artist" then. I only knew that when I grew up I would have to work for a living, and that I was going to work with a brush and a pencil and papers and do pictures. That's how I would have put it then.

LSM: Did you speak German at home?

EC: My parents spoke German to me, but I answered in English. When we went to Germany, I could understand my relatives, but I couldn't answer them.

LSM: Oh, I see! [both laugh]

EC: Quite quickly, though, within a short time, I was speaking German.

L S M : Was it following your first-grade year that you and your family went over to Germany?

E C : Actually, as it turned out, I went to first grade for about half of the year in Syracuse. I didn't know that until just recently, when we found my first-grade report card and the name of my teacher, Miss Frickey.

L S M : Did you have many children's books at home?

E C : No, I didn't. I had a Mickey Mouse book, I remember, and I loved *Flash Gordon* comic books. You know those fat, small books, which are now collectors' items. I was terribly intrigued by Flash Gordon and, even more so by the beautiful women in these stories! He was always rescuing some damsel in distress. I remember certain pages as vividly as when I first looked at them.

In one scene, Flash Gordon is traveling in an airplane, and a meteorite slashes through the wings. There is also a beautiful woman in the plane, and since only he has a parachute, he holds her tight so that they can parachute down together to safety. There I was, only four, five years old, and I liked such things!

L S M : Did you go to the movies?

E C : Yes. My father would take me to see any movie about nature. He loved animals. He also liked to take me for walks in the woods. In Syracuse my parents belonged to a nature club, and on the weekends we'd all go out to the Finger Lakes, where there were log cabins and boats. I remember on one such outing catching a snake that scared the other adults. But then my father stepped in and explained that it was only a harmless garter snake.

L S M : You sometimes put snakes in your books. Yours are never too frightening, but they usually come as a surprise.

E C : Yes, I suppose that's true.

L S M : It struck me just now as you described that incident with the snake that you had enjoyed getting a rise out of the grown-ups.

EC: Could be! [both laugh] All children like to do that.

In Germany, where the forests are more cultivated than here, with paths winding through the woods and then opening onto beautiful meadows, we would go hiking every weekend until I was ten, when my father was drafted into the army at the beginning of World War II. Even if we just walked a few steps from our own house we came to a brook, which we could follow out into the meadows and then on into the forest. If we kept on going we eventually came out at a castle.

LSM: It all sounds like a dream—or a German fairy tale. Was there a spiritual quality to the love of nature shared by your parents and their friends?

EC: My mother was the more practical, realistic type, but, yes, I think my father was a very spiritual man, though I didn't know it at the time. I would also describe him as a very intelligent but also a nonambitious man.

LSM: He was content with the work that he was doing?

EC: He was a clerk with the City Health Department—and I don't think he particularly enjoyed it. It was a dumb job, really. But he liked people, and they liked him, so that made it bearable. The rest was routine. It paid the rent.

LSM: Were your parents religious in the traditional sense?

EC: No. We were of Protestant background, but no one in my family went to church, not even my grandparents. In fact I wasn't baptized. Religion meant nothing to us. On the other hand, we didn't look down on it either, any more than up. It was just meaningless to us.

As it happened, we lived next door to the church, and often the preacher passed by and he and my mother would chat with each other. My mother would always slip him five marks for the church [both laugh] to pay off her guilt, I think, for not going!

LSM: At the time you went to Germany there were many Germans living here in this country, and there were people in Germany who had recently come from America. So, in a sense, as the war approached and then began, the two countries were more closely linked than one might have thought.

EC: Yes, that's very true. In the suburb of Stuttgart where we lived, there were a number of people with relatives who had come back to Germany from America. My father hadn't wanted to return to Germany. But my mother had become homesick after my Carle grandmother from Germany had visited us in Syracuse in 1934. And so it was decided to go. Of course, they later regretted it.

LSM: You've written about your new school as being very different from the one you attended in Syracuse.

EC: Yes, I hated the school in my new country.

LSM: How did you cope?

EC: By blending in—so well in fact that my teachers barely noticed me. I have described the corporal punishment aspect of that school's philosophy of education. I think I turned off in the face of that and decided to just get by.

LSM: As a child, did you know the classic German children's picture book *Struwwelpeter?* Readers have always had such extreme reactions to the book, finding it either utterly terrifying or hilariously funny.

EC: I loved it. Most psychologists and psychiatrists who work with children, educators—the official people—reject that book. Kids love it. It's outrageous, often cruel and fear-inducing, and full of exaggeration—a child's thumb gets cut off, another child burns to death, and yet another one starves himself to death! I find that you cannot be very subtle in your humor with children. Children often seem to enjoy these spine-tingling "cheap thrills" because deep down they know that these stories are invented, that the humor,

Eric Carle •

depiction of cruelty, and the fierce creatures are only in our imagination. Subtlety, on the other hand, may confuse the child. It has to be slapstick, and *Struwwelpeter* is slapstick—as are Mickey Mouse and Flash Gordon. It's so exaggerated that children know it's not true. Exaggeration takes the edge off. The same can be said of *Where the Wild Things Are*.

LSM: In *Rooster's Off to See the World* (1987) you provided a note saying that as a child you were more of a philosopher than a mathematician. Do you remember that?

EC: Yes, it had to do with my teacher trying to explain subtraction by speaking of "taking away an apple." My response at the time was that you cannot really take an apple away. You can hide it, you can put it behind your back, but then everyone knows it's behind your back.

LSM: Was there a hint of rebelliousness in your not wanting subtraction to work in the prescribed way?

EC: I don't know. I think my rebellion was an internal one. I had had this wonderful gentle teacher in Syracuse who formed the foundation, and when I went to Germany an old-fashioned disciplinarian teacher tried to tear it down. At some point, I must have decided that he was not going to win against me. That is my nature. I'm stubborn on certain issues.

LSM: You continued to draw and paint?

EC: Yes, always, and my parents were very supportive. When my relatives came visiting, they brought me pencils and watercolors and brushes. My mother would proudly show my work to visitors, and they would praise it.

LSM: She had taken to heart what your first teacher had told her.

EC: Absolutely. Otherwise, however, my mother was Germanic—somewhat dictatorial and domineering. In Germany, at that time, the idea was that a child had to be broken in by the time he or she was six years old. It was terrible. It's how the teachers thought, why mine felt justified in administering corporal punishment. He decided this free-spirited little American kid had to be broken in. He saw it as his duty.

LSM: Was there a certain point when you realized your family would not be returning to America?

EC: Yes, and that is when I decided I would become an engineer and build a bridge across the Atlantic. Looking back at my life, I think I have done so through my books. I say many critical things about Germany, but I also love Germany. But there are certain facts about Germany's history that one cannot overlook.

LSM: As a child who was visually oriented, did you notice the Nazi propaganda posters? They must have been posted everywhere.

EC: I did. In Europe, newspapers were publicly displayed in glass cases for all to read. I remember looking at those, too. I also remember Herr Heller's shop being destroyed on Crystal Night, in November 1938, when I was nine years old. As I walked past it on my way to school, I saw that the shop windows were bashed in and a policeman was standing guard, who told me to move on and go to school. And, I suppose, I forgot about it. But did I? We are talking about it. I feel ashamed that it didn't make more of an impression on me then, that I wasn't outraged. I have discussed this with my wife, who is an early childhood specialist, and she says that it might be too much to expect from a child of that age.

LSM: When you moved to Germany, it would seem from what you have written that the other children took a special interest in you at first because you were an American. Did those same children turn against you when America became the enemy?

EC: America never really became the enemy.

LSM: What do you mean?

EC: Even during the war, the Germans, I think, always looked up to

Eric Carle

the English and the Americans, especially the Americans. I know people won't believe that. The German propaganda of that time depicted the Russians as subhuman beings, the Poles as having no class, the Balkan peoples as primitive peasants, and the French as degenerates. But they admired the English and the Americans. Sure, America was about jazz and chewing gum and Hollywood. But it was also about big power, industrial might. They respected power. The sun never set on the British Empire, and so on. In school we learned English and studied English history, culture, and litera-ture—Shakespeare, for example.

LSM: How did you meet the first of the German teachers to have a great positive influence on you, Herr Krauss?

EC: In Germany children went to grammar school for four years, until the age of ten. Then a choice was made—whether you would go on to higher education or become, say, an apprentice mason, or railroad worker, or whatever. If you and your family chose a more advanced education, you would go eight more years to Gymnasium, or high school, which is what I did. That's where I met Herr Krauss. He was my art teacher, and he was a fabulous guy.

LSM: You have written that he spoke to you about your "free and sketchy style" of drawing.

EC: Yes, he pointed it out to me.

LSM: So you had an artistic style by the time you were ten! You have also written that Herr Krauss expressed his distaste for the propa-gandistic and naturalistic styles of art that were dominant in Ger-many during the Nazi period.

EC: It was all so heavy: the flag, the raised fist and the raised hand, and the soldiers and the workers and the farmers and the proud Ger-mans. On a more sentimental level there might also be an image of the sun setting on a farm. There was this strange combination of images of sentiment and images of power. Herr Krauss, however, had hung out and studied with the German Expressionists, whose art the Nazis condemned as "degenerate," and was forbidden to be shown or exhibited. On top of that, he had belonged to the Socialist Youth Movement. He must have been a pretty Bohemian-intellectual-artist type in his youth. Later, he had a family to support, and so he became an art teacher. He did not agree with what was going on, but like many people he felt he had to shut up about it.

I don't remember art classes in grammar school, but in Gymnasium, art classes were organized, and I was happy making pictures. Herr Krauss sensed some potential in me; he knew more about me than I knew about myself. That is why he asked me one day to come to his house, where he showed me reproductions of Expressionist and abstract paintings. That was when he pointed out the loose and sketchy quality of my own work, and when I heard him call the Nazis "charlatans" and "*Schweine*," which was utterly amazing—a very dangerous thing for him to do. These so-called "degenerate" paintings didn't make that much of an impression on me at the time, but I did come away with a certain strange feeling that I could not put into words.

LSM: Yet you still remember his exact words now!

EC: Yes, that's true. At the time, I must have thought he was crazy: What does he know?

LSM: Would you say that he risked his life by inviting you over?

EC: I certainly think so. As a Socialist and an Expressionist, he already had two strikes against him. If I had turned him in, something that I didn't even think of, he would have been interviewed by some horrible official person, who would have brought out his past, his mistakes, and next thing you know he might have been sent to a concentration camp. Those things happened, as I now know. After all, he didn't know me well. I was just one of his students, and we were all so idealistic: we thought we were good people. For Herr Krauss to contradict our reality was definitely a very dangerous move.

Now, when I visit my sister in Germany, I always drive through the village where he lived and say, "Oh, Herr Krauss lived around the corner." I visited him several times in later years, long after I had come back to live in the States. The last time I saw him he was retired and had gone senile. He didn't recognize me. His house-keeper had prepared for him a little basket with his medicine and an apple along with his pipe and tobacco, and he just shuffled around with it. He was painting a very neat and conventional little painting of sunflowers and—this is the funny part—he raged against abstract artists. In his senility, he considered *them* total charlatans.

LSM: You enrolled in art school after the war?

EC: In 1945, immediately after the war, Germany was still in chaos. All of the schools had been closed down. They had either been bombed out or could no longer be heated because of coal and oil shortages, or the teachers had to undergo the de-Nazification process. For the first six months after the war I worked as a filing clerk, for the American military government, to earn some money. After that, I returned to school and disliked it more than ever. So, I went to Herr Krauss for advice about my future, which I knew had to be in an art-related field. He made a list of the possibilities: window decorator, painter, theater designer, all the artistic professions. Then he added "graphic designer" to the list and said, "These people make the most money." That sealed my fate! [both laugh] He then recommended that I go see Professor Ernst Schneidler, head of the Graphic Arts Department of the *Akademie der Bildenden Künste* (Academy of Art and Design) in Stuttgart. My family, you see, wouldn't let me go to school to become just an artist. They were very practical. But graphic design was another matter. *That* was a profession, and it was fine with me, too. So off I went. I was sixteen years old. Here in the United States, it could be said that I dropped out of high school.

I studied with a man who was considered one of Germany's finest teachers in the field. Professor Schneidler was also known by connoisseurs of the graphic arts as the designer of several well-known typefaces, among other things. My father was away, in a prisoner-of-war camp in the Soviet Union, from which he didn't return until late 1947. In Herr Schneidler I finally found someone I could look up to, someone who understood me.

After my talk with Herr Krauss about my future, my mother and I decided that I would enroll at the Academy. In 1946, my mother accompanied me to go see Professor Schneidler. I was admitted at an exceptionally early age. Professor Schneidler looked at my portfolio and accepted me without requiring that I take the usual test. He also waived two other standard requirements—*Abitur,* an equivalent to a high school diploma, and a finished apprenticeship in the profession of the graphic arts, as a printer, lithographer, or typesetter. This went to my head! I thought I was this hot shit. [both laugh] I became an *artiste.* I was insufferable, and my work suffered as a result. So at the end of the first semester, he asked me to see him in his office. He called me on the carpet, saying that he wanted to kick me out of the school. But the next day I went back to talk to him, asking that he change his mind. He then told me that for the next three semesters I would be assigned to the typesetting shop as an apprentice. The typesetting shop was a part of the Graphic Arts Department. Herr Veith would be my teacher. He was an old traditionalist who could have come straight from the typesetting shop of Gutenberg. He lived and breathed type, typesetting, and typography. And I would be an apprentice and set type by hand for the next three semesters.

LSM: You make it sound like the equivalent of digging ditches.

EC: It was like digging ditches—and it was a stroke of genius on Professor Schneidler's part. That kind of disciplined training was just what I needed if I was going to go on developing my talent.

LSM: Did Professor Schneidler warm up to you later?

EC: I would see him in the hallway and, of course, we Germans were always very formal about addressing our professors. I would say, "Professor Schneidler, how are you?" "Oh, fine, Herr Carle. How's your mother?" "Good." For the next year and a half, that was the extent of our relationship. Finally, however, I went to see him and said, "Herr Professor, my three semesters are up. I hope you will critique my work again, and that I will be admitted again to the art classes." He agreed to do so, and from that moment onward we had a wonderful relationship.

He was a difficult man. We called him "The *Meister*"—and he was the master. He only came in once or twice a week for an hour or two and, in fact, said very little. He would look at a piece of work and say, "Dumb" or "Not dumb." Yet for forty years, he produced many of Germany's leading graphic artists, type designers, poster and book designers, illustrators, and art teachers. He somehow made us want to please him.

He would speak about "our cause," by which he meant our responsibility as designers to create better surroundings for people: a pleasing fabric for a jacket, a striking poster for a public space, a good typeface for reading, a satisfying design for a cup. This was our cause. I remember him saying that we were not going to change the world, but that we should think of ourselves as a link in a chain— an important link in society. That was his first message. After that, it was all about composition and color and design. He always spoke of being "decent" in our approach to design—that is, about being sure that we had aesthetic integrity—and about the ends to which we applied our talent.

LSM: That is fascinating to consider as a reaction or postcript to the legacy of the Nazi era.

EC: I still feel that I learned my most basic professional values from him. That is what made him a master. His students still occasionally meet to talk about him. It's almost like a knighthood to have been his student. I taught one year at Pratt in 1963 as a guest lecturer, and the attitude then was that the students expected the professor to please, to entertain them. When I went to school, it was the other way around: I was there to please Professor Schneidler, to gain his respect.

LSM: Did he give exercises or assignments?

EC: Not many.

LSM: What exactly did he do, then?

EC: He discovered each student's talent and nurtured it. Some students were good in calligraphy and others in poster design, and he would channel those talents. But most of all, he somehow instilled a certain spirit in us. This will sound crazy, but it was almost a religious experience.

It was during this period of my life that I finally separated from my family, who were tradespeople, clerks, laborers, bakers, butchers, tinsmiths. We didn't have many books. My mother went to one opera when she was eighteen years old, a performance of *La Bohème*—and talked about it for the rest of her life. My parents read little. And then there I was in Schneidler's class with, first of all, Schneidler himself, this magnificent man, as my mentor, and with all my fellow students from all walks of life, and with the knowledge of those who had come before us and gone on to do great things. A new world had opened up to me. They became my family. Even now the spirit of Schneidler is with me: The Force is with me! [both laugh]

LSM: What kinds of artwork were you doing at that time?

EC: Remember, we were engaged in graphic design and applied arts. Art per se was not the goal. We started out with exercises in "dividing space" or composition. For that part of our work, we would make up our own colored papers. For instance, we'd take a pot of red paint and a pot of yellow paint. Then we'd paint a sheet of pure red, followed by a sheet of red with one or maybe two drops of yellow, gradually increasing the yellow until we arrived at a sheet of almost pure yellow. Then we would work with green and black, blue and orange, and so forth. In this way, we accumulated a great many sheets of different colored papers, which we then would cut or tear into pieces, and arrange in mostly abstract patterns and designs. We then placed a mat around our compositions and put a piece of glass over them to hold them in place for Schneidler to view and critique. We didn't glue the papers down: the idea was just to train our sense of shape and color and composition, not to create something permanent. We regularly practiced this particular exercise throughout the four years. It was the equivalent, I suppose, of a pianist's scales.

From there it was on to calligraphy, bookbinding, lithography, photography, typography, printing, etching, woodcut and linoleum cut, poster design, illustration. After my stint at the typesetting shop, I did some linoleum cuts that Professor Schneidler looked at—and you know what he said? "Good!" Usually, as I told you earlier, it was either "Dumb" or "Not dumb." "Good" meant exceptional! Right away, however, he tempered his high praise. He said, in his precise Prussian accent, "That's good, all right. But, ah! You don't even understand why it's good." [both laugh] He meant for me to find out the "why." That, I think, was good advice.

LSM: So he kept you on edge.

EC: Yes, and then I did several etchings, and they did not turn out so good. I was not so good with the thin lines. My strength has always been in big, bold shapes. So with the etchings, it was back to "Not so good, not so good. Dumb, dumb." When we did calligraphy, he watched me for three months, and finally he said, "Herr Carle, not so good. Dumb. Don't do that anymore. Anyway, we don't need more calligraphers!"

LSM: And so he pointed you.

EC: Yes, and with his guidance a great many of us became strong and capable at one specialty or another.

LSM: Did you feel as though you were being initiated into a tradition?

EC: Yes, I did. For instance, when my typography teacher was a young man, there were still journeymen in Germany, as there had been since the Middle Ages. First there would be a three-year apprenticeship, and then you became a journeyman. A journeyman would walk say from Stuttgart to the next town, and to the next town, looking for work in the shop of a master, wearing a certain scarf or hat, or carrying a walking stick that identified his trade. And then finally, after many years, if he qualified, he might become a master himself. This system of training hardly existed by the time I was growing up, but through my typography teacher I had contact with the last generation of these journeymen. I think that a little of that tradition was passed on to me.

LSM: The term "international style" is often applied to postwar developments in architecture and design. Did you feel a part of that emerging tradition, too?

EC: Yes. For us in Germany it was very exciting because for twelve years, during the Nazi regime, so much had been repressed in art and design. I remember seeing experimental movies, for instance, some consisting strictly of abstract shapes, and thinking they were wild. I hadn't known such things could be done.

Having experienced that horrible war, we also realized what

nationalism could lead to, and so we became internationalists—at least, the artists, the designers, and the thinkers did. We felt very much like pioneers.

LSM: Then, in 1952, you returned to the United States.

EC: I always knew I would come back to America, but I felt I needed some professional experience first. So I worked for one year as a freelance poster designer for the United States Information Agency, and a second year as art director at a fashion magazine. By then, I had my portfolio and felt confident enough to return.

When as a greenhorn I arrived in New York City, I wanted to find a job as a graphic designer, preferably in advertising. Someone suggested that I go see the New York Art Directors' Show, which was on exhibit at the time. There I discovered the beautiful designs for *Fortune* magazine, for which Leo Lionni was the art director. Immediately after I left the exhibit, I called him on the telephone and asked if I could show him my work. He told me to come the next day at eleven o'clock. Mr. Lionni looked through my portfolio and arranged a meeting for me with George Krikorian, the art director for the Promotion Department of *The New York Times,* where Mr. Lionni knew of a job opening. I got the job! Leo Lionni became the next in the line of people who helped me professionally. Several years later, after he had created his own picture books, he encouraged me to do picture books, too. In two successive years, he set up appointments for me to see his editor. But both times, nothing came of it. It was much later, through Bill Martin Jr., that my career as a picture book artist began.

LSM: On leaving Europe for America, did you feel you were coming to a less cultured part of the world?

EC: Not at all. When the war broke out and for some time after the war had ended, there was no opportunity for me as a young man to absorb the famous European culture, the magnificent cathedrals and the art, to visit the great museums. But then when I came to New York, I went to the Museum of Modern Art, the Metropolitan Museum of Art, and this was more culture than I had ever experienced.

LSM: Soon after your return, however, you were drafted into the United States Army. When you returned to civilian life, you continued to work for the *Times* and then went on to work for an advertising agency specializing in pharmaceutical advertising. Did your experience as an advertising artist serve you well when you later turned to children's book illustration?

EC: In advertising, you try to surprise, be different. If everyone uses big type, you use small type. If everybody uses red, you use green, not because green is better than red, but because it will stand apart. In advertising, surprise and shock are important. In advertising, you can shock or you can be extremely tasteful, or you can combine the two!

LSM: You've never been shocking in your books, though, have you?

EC: Not I suppose until *Draw Me a Star* (1992), in which I painted Adam and Eve as a nude couple. I got a little flak for that, but I still don't consider it daring. One teacher wrote to say, "Your grandmother would be ashamed of you." [both laugh] But it really was so mild.

LSM: Why did you leave advertising?

EC: Advertising is a profession for young men and women. At the age of forty you ought to be a partner or own your own business or be the manager or executive or something, and that's exactly what happened with me. I had started out as a designer at the agency, and frankly I was doing fine work there. Then I got the very glamorous title of international art director. We had overseas offices, and it became my job to set up our art departments in all of them. I was still in my early thirties, and all that traveling seemed very exciting to me. Then, one day, I found I did not want to do it anymore. All too often I had to go out with clients, have dinner and drinks with them, attend meetings, and there was all the backstabbing and office intrigue. It just hit me one day that all I wanted to do was to make pictures.

LSM: You remind me now of your book *A House for Hermit Crab* (1988). You knew it was time to move on.

EC: I suppose that's true. I'm a Cancer, born in June: that's the sign of the crab. And I myself am somewhat of a hermit. In general, I'd much rather stay at home and work in my garden than travel. Also, I suppose, the message of that book is the lesson that Professor Schneidler gave his students: start anew, move on, keep surprising.

LSM: You met Bill Martin Jr. around the time you left the advertising agency, did you not?

EC: I illustrated his *Brown Bear, Brown Bear, What Do You See?* (1967). I had already been thinking of quitting when I met Bill, who was employed at the time as an editor and writer at Henry Holt, where he created a line of books for the school market, not for the trade.

Bill's version of how we met is that he was at his doctor's office, leafing through one of the medical magazines, when he saw an ad I had designed featuring a collage illustration of a lobster. He told his art director to find the artist who had done that ad. In my version, I was getting ready to freelance and left my portfolio one day with his art director, who showed it to Bill. His story's more colorful than mine, but I think mine is the truth!

In any case, that was a lucky combination—Bill Martin Jr. and Eric Carle. A few years ago we traveled together on a book-signing tour and got to know each other better. One morning he came down from his hotel room to breakfast and said, "Eric, what do you think of this? 'Da da da da da DAH.' Or should it be: 'da da DAH da da

DAH?'" "Bill, what are you talking about?" I asked. "Oh, my next book. I usually do the rhythm first, before I do the words." Isn't that wonderful? Therein lies the secret of his success. His books are *all* rhythm—heartbeat!

LSM: What else did you learn about writing picture books from him?

EC: Bill opened the world of picture books for me when I illustrated *Brown Bear, Brown Bear, What Do You See?* For one thing, I learned the value of repetition and rhythm. That lesson stood me in good stead when I came to write the text of *The Very Hungry Caterpillar* (1969).

Before I met him, I had been given a freelance assignment by an educational publisher for which I was asked, in essence, to illustrate thirty-two good ideas on a single page. My reaction was that I would rather take one good idea and illustrate it across thirty-two pages. Bill's philosophy of the picture book was the same as mine.

LSM: Then you met Ann Beneduce, who has remained your editor all these years.

EC: The first book I brought her was *1, 2, 3 to the Zoo* (1968). I was being very careful. It was like dipping my big toe in the water. It was a wordless book; I had stayed away from language because I didn't yet trust myself to write. It was a conventional counting book, you know the kind, with one elephant, two giraffes, and so forth. Ann looked it over and said, "There are many children's counting books. We have to give this something extra to take it out of the ordinary. You can do it!" That was all she said.

So I went home and added the little train on the bottom in the gatefold. That was the next lesson I learned: have something extra. When it came to *The Very Hungry Caterpillar*, Ann didn't have to say, "Add holes." I had done a dummy, with holes and all, for that book before I met her. It originally was going to be called *A Week with Willi Worm!* I worked on it with Ann, who first suggested a caterpillar instead of a worm, and who, of course, published it.

LSM: Children aren't supposed to punch holes in their books. Did you feel that by adding the die-cut holes in *The Very Hungry Caterpillar* you were introducing an element of mischief into your work?

EC: Perhaps, without realizing it. But I thought of the holes primarily as a design element. I always try to squeeze as much as possible out of the paper. If possible, I don't want just a plain sheet of paper. I often want to have a fold or a hole or other device. I want to change that flat sheet any way I can. That is how the designer in me came to do holes.

LSM: You have also talked about wanting to make books that are also toys.

EC: That impulse comes from my observation that up to a point a child is more tactile than verbal: holding hands, holding his or her bottle or rattle, and being held is what matters to them at first. School comes later, and with school comes sitting still and focusing on the words in books. So I thought there should be something between the warmth of being held and of holding on to a toy, and the more abstract experience of book learning. There should be a bridge between—and that is what I've tried to create in the form of a book with holes in it, for example, a book that is partly also a toy. It is a toy you can read, and a book you can touch.

LSM: Why did you choose to illustrate your children's books in collage?

EC: In thinking about my books, I don't put too much emphasis on collage per se. It's just a technique. Some paint in oils, others in pen and ink. At least, that's how I see it. The reason I happen to do collage may, of course, go back to my art school experiences with Professor Schneidler, "dividing spaces" with the colorful papers which I created as an art student. That could be so.

LSM: Collage seems to be such a free-form medium.

EC: Well, yes and no. It's very free in that you can shift the papers around. But the shapes are very defined, and once they are glued down, their relationship to each other is also defined.

LSM: The article about your work in *Graphis* [volume 15, November 1959] refers to your interest in chance elements. Does that, too, go back to your classes with Professor Schneidler?

EC: Yes. Sometimes you have to listen to chance. You have to look at the crack in the wall. You might follow that crack and be surprised to find a picture in it. It's like the children's game of looking at a cloud and seeing an image, say a sheep, in the shape of the cloud.

In my studio, I have files full of my papers, hundreds and hundreds of tissue papers, all filed by color. I may take one that happens to be on the top, it will look good, and so I'll glue it down. That's the way it goes, often. Other times, it won't look good to me, and so I'll take out another paper and another. But often the one that pleases me just happens to be in the top of my drawer. I believe in chance. You carry a cup of coffee across a room. You look at it and it spills, or you don't look at it, and it doesn't spill. It's that type of chance event that I have in mind.

For instance, consider how this illustration emerged as the image of a porcupine in *Today Is Monday* (1993). I started by thinking, how am I going to do a porcupine? You see the gray paper here, the grayish paper? First I took a gray paper, then I went over it with black-and-white brushstrokes. From this I cut out the pieces for the quills. At that point, I didn't know what the quills would look like. It was unpredictable. I then cut out a dark blue shape for the porcupine's body and glued it down on a white board, and over the dark blue shape I glued the quills. I didn't know what would happen. I just had an idea it was going to work, and I was right in my assessment.

Other times it doesn't work. I'll have the same sort of impulse—

Eric Carle

that I should do this, this, and this, and then this, this, and this is going to happen. Only it doesn't happen at all. That's the chance of it.

In my picture of a porcupine, there must be a hundred quills, each individually pasted down. That takes a long time, but I enjoy doing it. I'm sort of suspended as I work. That's the most satisfying part of my work, I think, simply being in that state.

LSM: In the video you have made about your working methods, it looks as if making the papers is almost a meditation for you, to be putting the colors down and observing the patterns and effects as they play themselves out.

EC: Yes, it is. It's like being in an alpha state: total peace. Other artists must have the same sort of experience.

LSM: You have said that often the idea for a book forms in your mind rather quickly, and that it then often takes you another couple of years to work the idea out to your satisfaction.

EC: That's true, in general. I'll have a rough idea, just a seed, a beginning. In the case of *The Very Quiet Cricket* (1990), I simply decided that I wanted to do a book about a cricket. That was all I had at the beginning. In the case of *The Very Hungry Caterpillar*, all I knew was that I had the holes punched into a stack of papers. All I needed now was a "hero."

That doesn't mean I toil daily on a book. I might put an idea I've worked on away for two weeks or six months or a year or more, and then take it out again to work on it some more. The first dummies I make are quite rough, then they get neater and neater. Finally, I make one in color, in crayon maybe, for myself and to show my editor.

As I work on the book, I love it. I hate it. I think it's awful—and I think it's wonderful. I discuss it some more with my editor. Then there comes a time when I feel it's right: I don't know, but I feel it to be so. That's when I consider the book done.

LSM: Recently, you have started to do books that are more directly autobiographical.

EC: I tried to write a longer book, without pictures, about my boyhood in Germany during the war. I started to write it, but I found it very disturbing. I had nightmares about the war and tanks and people shooting at me. So I stopped and instead wrote *Flora and Tiger: 19 Very Short Stories from My Life* (1997). They're simple autobiographical stories, each somehow concerned with animals and insects, a relative or a friend, and me.

LSM: Would you tell me about your experiences visiting children in schools?

EC: I used to do a lot of that. After a while I could tell almost from the moment I entered a school what kind of principal it had. I found that the principal's spirit pervaded everything. I would walk in and say to myself, "This is a rigid school." Then I would actually meet the principal, and sure enough he or she would turn out to be a rigid person. Other schools would be just the reverse.

But let me tell you about the presentation I made. The children and I would pretend to do an illustration for a book together. I'd say, "What is your favorite animal?" Someone would answer, "Cats," so I would draw a cat's head. Then another child would say, "Giraffes," so I would add a giraffe's neck, and then as others spoke up asking for a turtle, I would add a shell, and so on. That presentation of mine, in fact, was the beginning of *The Mixed-Up Chameleon* (1975).

Here is another exercise that I did with children in their classroom. I would ask, "Do you think I can fool your eyes?" What happened next depended on how they answered. If they said, "No!" I'd know I hadn't made contact with them. But if the children shouted, "Yes, yes, you can fool our eyes!" this would mean that I had gained their confidence. I would then say, "What's the opposite of black?" They'd shout, "White!" Then I would ask, "What's the opposite of red?" After a brief pause, they would always say, with confusion in their voice, "What do you mean, what's the opposite of red?" That's when I would hold up a big red dot in front of a white wall and say, "Now stare at the red dot, and stare at it, and stare at it. Don't let your eyes wander at all, and watch what happens when I pull away the red dot. Watch carefully. Another color will appear, and that is the opposite—or complementary—color of red." When I pulled the red dot away, they continued to look and look and, finally, very tentatively, someone would always say, "Green?" After that the children felt confident that they too had seen the green afterimage. By the way, this exercise is based on Goethe's Color Theory. It became the basis for my book *Hello, Red Fox* (1998).

LSM: Ann Beneduce was also the first American editor to publish the work of Mitsumasa Anno. Do you know his books?

EC: Oh, I love his work. He's one of my absolute favorites. Ann introduced me to him once in London. His books and mine are very different, yet our goals are the same.

LSM: Anno said something to me that I thought summed up a lot about his work. He said that he wanted his books to "teach without teaching."

EC: That is what I attempt to do also. I would put it a little differently. I would say that I camouflage my teaching. Yes, I camouflage mine.

LSM: I also wonder whether you are acquainted with Margaret Wise Brown's books?

EC: I had seen *Goodnight Moon* before I began doing my own books. As an adult who was not particularly interested in picture books, I didn't quite understand the appeal of *Goodnight Moon*. It seems to me that adults don't always appreciate the artistry of picture books, especially the picture books for preschoolers and just-about readers.

And early on, I, too, thought, "What's so great about *Goodnight Moon*?" Later as I began to do my own books, I realized the depth and mastery of Margaret Wise Brown's work. I now know why children respond to her work with all their hearts and souls. And that brings me to an interesting point. It was the children who embraced my work to begin with, not the adults. I still feel that teachers and librarians would not be aware of my work were it not for the many children who wanted to look at and read my books and take them out of the library. That's what Margaret Wise Brown and I have in common: children have chosen us, not the professionals, not the librarians, or the teachers, or the grandmothers. I don't just think that, I *know* it to be so.

LSM: How has your work as a picture book artist changed over the years?

EC: It has become more painterly—and after so many years I would think it also should be better. When I visit museums now, I look less at a painting as a whole. Instead, I get intrigued by the textures created by the brushstrokes on the canvas or by the patterns in the grass or in the leaves or brickwork or water. Seen that way, a painting becomes an abstraction. I'm especially fascinated by the brushstrokes, dots, and patterns of the Impressionists—Renoir, Seurat, Monet, Degas, and don't forget van Gogh. I focus entirely on the brushstrokes or, say, on a certain pattern of dots. Inspired, I return to my studio and paint more of my papers.

....

Tana Hoban

Born ?
Philadelphia, Pennsylvania

....

*T*ana Hoban grew up in and around Philadelphia, the eldest of three children of Russian and Ukranian Jewish immigrants. She enrolled in art school intending to draw and paint but later found herself concentrating increasingly on photography. On graduation, she pursued her newfound interest in both the commercial and fine-art worlds. Starting in the 1940s, Hoban's photographs appeared in Good Housekeeping, Ladies' Home Journal, and other important national magazines. During the 1950s, after presenting her work to the legendary photographer and curator Edward Steichen, she twice had photographs selected for exhibitions at the Museum of Modern Art.

In 1970, when Hoban published her first children's picture book, Shapes and Things, books for the very young were receiving increased attention. Photography, however, was still viewed by many in the field as a literal-minded medium of illustration, ill-suited to stimulating children's imagination. Against this mixed background, Hoban's visually striking and thought-provoking "concept books" came as a revelation. Shapes and Things and her many subsequent books proved decisively photography's power not only to "copy" reality but also to encourage in viewers a heightened level of awareness.

Hoban, whose brother Russell Hoban is the author of the Frances
books for children *and such novels as* Riddley Walker, *has for many
years lived in Paris. She was in New York to deliver the dummy of her
picture book* More, Fewer, Less *(1998), when we recorded this interview at the offices of her longtime publisher, Greenwillow Books, on
August 27, 1997.*

LEONARD S. MARCUS: When you go out with your camera for a
walk, what do you hope to find?

TANA HOBAN: I used to carry a camera everywhere. Now it's gotten
heavier—so I carry a smaller one! More often than not, I go out now
specifically looking for pictures for a book I'm working on. Many
times I'm working on two books simultaneously and will be shooting for both. I'll go down the streets and visit the kinds of places
that I think children can identify with, and sometimes the same
scene will be good, say, for shapes and for colors. Maybe one time
I'll be counting everything; another time I'll be looking for circles
and squares.

I'm always looking for images for my *Look* book series. It's exciting to find subjects that work for one of those books.

LSM: Do you test the *Look* book photographs by putting them
behind a small opening, to see whether it's possible to readily identify the subject?

TH: Yes. That's how I started on those books. I happened to have a
cutout of a circle or a square in my studio and, by chance, left it
lying on top of a picture. Then I looked at it, also by chance, and
thought, Oh, here's an idea for a book!

LSM: *Look Again!* (1971) was one of your earliest children's books.

TH: When I showed my dummy for *Look Again!* to Susan Hirschman,
who was then the editor at Macmillan, her first response was that it

Tana Hoban

might be too gimmicky. She said, "See what else you can do," and gave me a definite date by which to call her. So the following week I showed her a dummy for *Shapes and Things,* a book of photograms, which Macmillan published first.

A photogram is made by putting an object on the paper, shining the light on it, and then printing the resulting image as you would an ordinary enlargement. Photograms are so easy to make that I thought for sure someone else would have the same idea. So I worked night and day to get the book done.

LSM: You photographed your first books in black and white. Was working in color an option for you then?

TH: No, it wasn't. I don't know whether it was the expense of printing in color or what. Later, when I was told I could use color in books, I began to do so. Black and white can be richer than color, because it's so graphic. But color, of course, is the way we see.

LSM: Do you still recall taking the photographs for *Look Again!?*

TH: Absolutely. I was living in Philadelphia at the time. I found the little zebra at the Philadelphia Zoo. I think that that must have been the first image I did for the book. Those stripes are so strong graphically.

I did the photograph of the pear in my studio. My mother always cut an apple across so that we would see the star shape inside. As a child I would cut pears for my younger sister, just as you see the one in my photograph: I would take the top, the cone shape, and she would get the bottom.

LSM: Do you often feel as you work that you are photographing images remembered from your childhood?

TH: Yes, often. We lived in the country, and my early love of nature is certainly reflected in my books. Growing up, we had lots of animals—dogs and cats and pigeons and squirrels. I always have animals in my books. My father and mother raised white pigeons—

at one time we had five thousand of them—and since then I have always been fascinated by the pigeons I see in the park because of the beautiful designs on their backs. I photographed a group of pigeons for *Look Book* (1997).

I love doing the *Look* books. Children are so pleased that they know the answers. I have found that they also enjoy repeatedly going through the pictures, to see if anything has changed!

LSM: Were there books that you considered special when you were a child?

TH: No, but my father told us many traditional Russian stories, such as the one about it being so cold outside that birds dropped frozen from the sky. I think all Russian Jewish children knew that story. My father was a Socialist, and he also told us the one about the heroic engineer who sees something up ahead on the tracks, stops the train, then cuts his arm to make his shirt turn red, so he'll be able to stop the next train!

My brother, Russell, recalls that at dinner, my father had a glassful of nickels that he would give us children for clever remarks. Talking with my sister at the dinner table one evening, I apparently said, *"N'est-ce pas?"* And when she asked, "What's that?" I replied, "An old French general." Then my brother chimed in with, "Tecumseh!" And when I asked, "What's that?" he answered, "An old Indian chief!" He got a nickel for that remark. We both got nickels.

LSM: Did you have a camera when you were young?

TH: Not as a child, though my father had a large Graflex. There was flash powder, and there would be a big boom. Very dramatic! My father wasn't a photographer, however. He was advertising manager at *The Jewish Daily Forward.*

As a child I liked to draw and decided early on to become an artist. Later, when I went to art school, I studied photography and,

Tana Hoban

in what felt like a strange coincidence, was given a Graflex like my father's to work with.

LSM: Were there certain photographers whose work you felt influenced by or admired early on?

TH: Of course there was Edward Weston and Edward Steichen, whose photographs had a poetic quality I liked. I showed Steichen my photographs and was included in a group show of women photographers that he curated at the Museum of Modern Art in 1949, as well as in the museum's *Family of Man* exhibition of 1955.

LSM: Did you know the two books that Steichen photographed for young children, *The First Picture Book* (1930) and *The Second Picture Book* (1931)?

TH: Yes, but I couldn't say whether I saw them before or after I began doing my own books.

LSM: Certainly your picture books have an affinity with the Steichen books as attempts to offer the very young compelling images of everyday objects and activities.

TH: Yes, it has been my idea, too, to photograph everyday things that a child can relate to, as a vehicle for learning. Simple, generic things. Not Mickey Mouse!

LSM: How did the children's book world strike you as compared with the world of advertising, in which you were then still immersed?

TH: I continued to work in advertising until I had published ten or so books. It was very different. The stress level in advertising was so much higher. You would get an assignment. You agreed on a price. Then you went and shot the assignment—and it might not come out at all right.

When I started out in photography after art school, I took pictures mainly for myself. I specialized in photographing children. I would find children I thought were photogenic and take them to the park, a natural setting, and try to get a spontaneous response. Instead of the typical Eastman Kodak look of the time, where the child was always blond, not Jewish, not black, not Italian, and not Chinese, and always smiling at the camera, I photographed a variety of children in more thoughtful, introspective moods. I wanted to show that childhood is not always the happy time it appears to be. Maybe the timing was right. My pictures were noticed and became known. Even the J. Walter Thompson advertising agency, which had such a big part in creating the visual stereotypes of that period through their various advertising campaigns, gave me a big show in their gallery. Then, I myself worked on the Kodak and Polaroid accounts.

LSM: Kodak, which you just mentioned in connection with the stereotyped images of childhood, became willing to try something different?

TH: Yes. They saw my pictures and liked what I did. But I always did photographs to please myself as well.

LSM: Your brother also worked in advertising, did he not?

TH: Yes, writing copy. He began doing children's books long before I did, but there has never been any connection between his work in the field and mine. For me, there was simply the natural progression of going from photographing children to photographing images for children and, in a sense, from the child's point of view.

LSM: What more specifically prompted you to try your hand at making children's picture books?

TH: I had read an article about an experiment at the Bank Street School in New York. When the teachers first asked the children what they saw every day on their way to school, the children replied, "Nothing." Then the children were all given cameras, and they suddenly discovered the rivers, the construction sites, the food stands they passed every day. Having a camera opened their eyes.

Reading about that experiment prompted me to wonder what things I was not seeing in the course of a day. I began to look at my surroundings differently.

LSM: Have ideas for books come to you in the same way?

TH: The idea for *26 Letters and 99 Cents* (1987) did. I had read somewhere that children should know the alphabet by such-and-such age and be able by then to make a certain amount of change—thirty-nine cents, I think it was. When I discussed my idea for a book based on this premise with Susan Hirschman, we decided to make it ninety-nine cents, a less arbitrary-sounding number that, even with inflation, would never make the book seem out-of-date.

LSM: You used a great many toys as subjects for the book. Do you collect toys?

TH: When I see something that isn't associated with a particular trade name or character or designer, something that can't be pinned down, I usually buy it. I had, for instance, bought a set of the lower case letters that I used for *26 Letters*. I also wanted a matching set of capital letters but found that there was none. So I tracked down the people who designed and manufactured the letters I already had—they were a young couple living in Bath, England—and commissioned them to make the capital letters for me. I felt that it was important to have the letters look as they do.

As for the other objects I photographed for the book, I simply chose things that I thought children would like: toy dinosaurs, dragons, robots, and cars. An egg. A goldfish. Jellybeans are pretty universal. The quilt I photographed was given to me as a wedding present by Greenwillow when I married the second time. I found the sea horse that I photographed on the beach years ago.

LSM: Do you spend much time arranging the objects in your photographs?

TH: Not a lot of time. The objects in my pictures for *Of Colors and Things* (1989), for example, are casually arranged. I don't want them to look perfectly styled as in an ad.

LSM: Do you take a great many pictures to produce a 32-page picture book?

TH: That depends. Take the cover photographs for *The Moon Was the Best* (text by Charlotte Zolotow, 1993). On the front cover I have a picture of a girl running away from the viewer. On the back I have exactly the same scene, with the girl running toward you. To get that pair of pictures took two whole days. I wanted it to look fresh and spontaneous! And I had to make sure no one else had wandered into the picture, and so on. In that case, I started out with a preconceived notion of what I wanted.

Other times, I'll have some such idea, but it will turn out not to be the picture I take, or eventually use. Something will turn up in a picture by chance that will be better than what I had imagined. For instance, when I was photographing *Look Again!* and first saw the peacock at the Philadelphia Zoo, his back was to me, and I thought I would just wait until he turned around. It had not occurred to me that I might want to photograph him from the back. But peacocks turn very slowly. They make a little dance of it. And as I continued to look at the outspread feathers from the back, I suddenly thought, Ah! That's the picture.

LSM: Do you take all the pictures for a book at the same time of day, or in the same kind of light, for the sake of visual continuity? Is lighting a part of a book's formal design?

TH: No, I don't worry about that. Most of my pictures are done in natural daylight, and if I use artificial light I do it in such a way as to imitate natural light.

LSM: How involved do you become in the design of your books?

TH: Very. My dummies look very much like the books that come out of them. Ava Weiss, the art director at Greenwillow (now retired), works out the precise details.

When I prepare my spreads, I put all the pictures on the floor and then pick them out two at a time and see how they look together. But I don't look for the "S-curve," or the "center of interest" that graphic designers talk about. It's all intuitive, and very often the first choice I make turns out to be right.

LSM: When your books are published abroad, do you sometimes have to replace photographs with others of subjects more familiar to the children of that country or part of the world?

TH: For the French edition of *26 Letters and 99 Cents* (*Des sous et des lettres*, Kaléidoscope, 1996), I photographed French coins. In the German edition of another book, I had to replace a photograph of a fire hydrant, because German children would have found it unrecognizable. There have been a few instances of that kind.

LSM: Except for *The Moon Was the Best*, with its views of Paris, your photographs don't generally call attention to the locales where they were taken.

TH: That's right. They could be anywhere. That's because I want them to be not so much about places as about seeing.

LSM: How did *Little Elephant* (1994), the first book written by your daughter, Miela Ford, come about?

TH: I often go to the Paris Zoo to photograph animals, and one day the baby elephant seemed to be acting exactly like a little child. I had never seen it behave that way before. I photographed as fast as I could! Usually the baby elephant would just be walking around, curling its trunk, doing the usual things. But that day, it took so many poses that it almost wrote the book for me. I went back the next day, and the elephant just stood around. It didn't do anything!

I say "almost wrote the book" because when I showed the photographs to Susan, she said that she loved the book, but that this time my pictures would need words to accompany them. She tried several writers who didn't work out. Then my daughter, who was already grown by the time I began making my first books, and who had never written before, said that she would like to try—and she did. Now she both writes and photographs her own books. I loved it that we had done a book together.

LSM: How has your work changed over the years?

TH: I used to photograph children. But in my picture books I don't often include children in the photographs. That is because I don't want to pin down just who the child of the book is; I want readers to put themselves in the book.

LSM: Your books relate so directly to the theories about developmental learning that originated at Bank Street and at some of the other centers of progressive education. Have you ever had a more formal association with any of those schools, or studied the work of, say, John Dewey or Lucy Sprague Mitchell?

TH: No. As I said earlier, I work very much by intuition. I don't test my books on children. I ask myself, Is it childlike? I do my work and know when it's right.

LSM: I have read that your books have been used with learning-disabled children.

TH: My books apparently work well with children with learning disabilities because there is no threat of the word on the page. If a picture comes with a caption, if a book says, "This is a such-and-such," there's a chance that the child may get it wrong. But if there is no word or caption, then a "car" can be an "auto," or a "means of transportation," or whatever the child thinks to call it. Having no words liberates a child to a certain extent. A picture by itself will elicit a personal response that will get him going. I like to think that my books provoke young children to talk—to express themselves.

. . . .

Karla Kuskin

Born July 17, 1932
New York, New York

······························

As a child, Karla Kuskin recalls, "poetry was an essential part of my diet." She liked to draw and paint as well, and as a graduate student at the Yale University School of Art, she combined these interests by creating her first picture book, Roar and More (1956), as a class project. Soon after graduation, Kuskin sold Roar and More to Harper & Brothers, thus launching herself on the career she has pursued ever since.

Kuskin's laserlike eye, wry sense of humor, and memory for childhood's emotional ups and downs inform and flavor her work as a poet and illustrator. She enjoys the company of cats in part because cats are such good observers, too. She has described herself as "an incurable keeper of things and memories; as you get older, I think they become each other."

Kuskin's poetry collections include The Rose on My Cake (1964), Near the Window Tree: Poems and Notes (1975), Soap Soup and Other Verses (1992), and The Sky Is Always in the Sky (1998). Her quiet mastery of poetic forms and devices has carried over into her prose writings, as in the subtly paced, rhythmic text of The Philharmonic Gets Dressed (1982). She has also taught writing workshops for schoolchild-

ren and written perceptively about children's literature for The New York Times Book Review *and other publications. In 1979, Kuskin received the National Council of Teachers of English Award for excellence in poetry for children, for the body of her work.*

Portions of this interview were recorded on September 14, 1998, and September 23, 1999, in Kuskin's Brooklyn, New York, home.

LEONARD S. MARCUS: What makes poetry for children different from other poetry?

KARLA KUSKIN: It is simpler, friendlier to children. It is written to accustom children to poetry as a form and to encourage their affection for it. Children love to read and to hear rhyme—although they're not good at writing rhyme. They're wonderful with imagery, and they respond to rhythm. All these considerations enter into my work when I'm writing poetry for them.

LSM: What were some of your own first experiences of poetry?

KK: My father, who wrote advertising copy for a living, was a versifier. He would make up poems for birthdays, Valentine's Day, and other special occasions. As my father played Rodgers & Hart at the piano, I would sit beside him and sing the lyrics, even though I couldn't carry a tune. I still can't.

Before I knew how to write I made up verses of my own. I dictated to my mother. She wrote them down, and I felt encouraged. Here's one of my earliest works:

> A gentleman went out for an airing.
> He forgot his hat.
> Oh Oh dear dear,
> What shall we do about that?

I can also remember some lines of a poem I must have written several years later, called "Grown-ups' Chatter"; this is a chorus:

> The war is on in Britain.
> The war is on in France.
> Oh what shall we do about Poland?
> Finland is in a terrible mess.
> Oh there goes Norway again.

My parents read poetry aloud to each other as well as to me. My teachers at the Little Red School House, in Greenwich Village, were very good readers, too. When I was seven, I was given a copy of *Old Possum's Book of Practical Cats,* which I loved and can still recite at length. As a child, I would be paid a nickel—and later a quarter—for supplying the headlines for certain ads for a men's tailor who was a client of my father's. That experience taught me to write short, to pare things down to the bare essence. So my childhood was filled with words and rhythmic language and a love of poetry.

LSM: You just quoted a poem of yours about World War II. Did the war make a deep impression on you as a child?

KK: I recall asking my mother whether there had been any news before the war began, because the war was all we heard about over the radio. At one time I kept a little bag packed just in case we had to leave our home in a hurry. At Little Red we sat indoors on the stairs and practiced putting our heads down on our knees, in case the bombers came. And when my Uncle Arnold went into the Army Air Force, I wore his insignia on my sweater, which made me feel very glamorous. But we never did see bombers overhead, and although I can't be sure of this, I don't think our dreams were filled with war. Even so, the war was brought home for me in other ways.

One of my dearest friends then and now is an American-born Japanese, and I was very aware of anti-Japanese feelings. I felt very protective of Ikuyo and her family.

LSM: Did you memorize much poetry as a child?

KK: The Little Red School House was a "progressive" school, which meant in part that our teachers were philosophically opposed to rote learning. We were, however, encouraged to read poems we liked to the class. As a result of that experience, my friend March and I began to read poetry to each other. This was when we were both about thirteen. I think one reason that some schoolchildren don't develop an affinity for poetry is that their teachers' first experiences with poetry involved rote memorization and analysis: "Memorize this, dissect that," instead of sheer enjoyment. That negative attitude continues to be passed on to the next generation.

LSM: Your school was loosely affiliated with the nearby Bank Street School, where Lucy Sprague Mitchell introduced the experientially based "here and now" approach to writing for young children, and guided the early writing careers of Margaret Wise Brown and Ruth Krauss, among others. Did the "here and now" idea leave a lasting impression on you or influence your work as a poet?

KK: Certainly the way I was taught as a young child left a lasting impression. We did concentrate first on learning about our surroundings and then branched out into the wider world. Once we were writing, we wrote journals, plays, etc., that related to the subject at hand. For example, when we studied Manhattan and learned about the old city of New Amsterdam, we walked around the neighborhood and noticed the Dutch-style roofs that could still be found near our school. We put on a play in which I, eight-year-old Karla Seidman, played Peter Stuyvesant, complete with a wooden leg. And a triumph it was, I might add! And we made candles and cooked food typical of the Dutch colony, and so on, until after a while those experiences became part of our own experience. When it came to our writing, what mattered most, perhaps, was that our teachers made us feel that what we, as children, had to say had value. That was a wonderful thing to realize.

The emphasis on the everyday also underlies a method I worked out for introducing poetry to schoolchildren. For some years I made annual visits to two schools in Texas, where I saw the same eight-, nine-, and ten-year-old classes each day for a week. I would begin by saying, "Write me a description of some familiar object. It can be very short, but don't just say that the thing you're writing about is pretty: I want to be able to see what you see and to know why you chose to write about it." When the children read their pieces to each other, it always turned out that their descriptions touched on their feelings about their subjects—a favorite doll or bear, for instance. So the second assignment would be to write a description that explored their feelings, more deliberately, about their subject. With each assignment, I added another of the elements that go into the making of a simple poem.

After feeling came memory. I told the children a memory of my own: "When I was little, I lived in an apartment on the top floor of a house. I had a little room, and every night when I got into bed there would be a fox under my bed. And the fox had a dumbwaiter (I explained what this was), and on this dumbwaiter were beautifully colored bottles, all filled with liquids, all of them poisonous. So I knew I had to lie in the exact middle of the bed, with my hands at my sides, or I would somehow be poisoned, and I would die." After telling this story, I asked if any of the children had similar memories of night frights. All but a very few of them did. A few who could not remember were children who had been so severely traumatized at some point that they had blocked out memories of their night fears altogether. And so I asked them just to make something up. That's how I introduced imagination to the group.

I have never asked children to write a poem. I think that's a big mistake. At no point have I asked children to rhyme or to follow a particular form, though it often turns out that their descriptions can, with the addition of a few line breaks, be made to look like poems. And if it looks like a poem and sounds like a poem, isn't it a poem?

LSM: Why not encourage rhyming? Why not ask directly for poems?

KK: Children have a fresh eye: it's that quality that we treasure in them and that we, as writers, hope to keep alive in ourselves. Children pay attention, and they don't edit their experiences to the extent that we all learn to do as we grow older. However, they do not have a broad enough range of language to rhyme creatively. As a result, they use other peoples' rhymes, and this leads to stale, predictable writing.

You want to create a situation in which the child is really struggling with words. For that reason, I would never hand a child a form, saying, for instance, "We need three adjectives, dear. Start with 'A rose is a . . .' and fill in the blanks." When you take that approach, you're making it too simple. You may get something that's nice to take home to Mommy, but you won't bring out what's inside the child's own imagination. But when a child just blurts out as simply as possible what he or she has to say on a certain subject, the blurt often comes out sounding like poetry to us.

LSM: What role does rhyme play in your poems?

KK: It gives a poem a scattering of little explosions—the kind of *zetz* that's also achieved by a strong punch line. Too tight a rhyme scheme can be boring, however.

Writing for me is a process of getting it right, of writing a sentence, reversing the order of the clauses or phrases, taking out the words that don't contribute, getting it down to the bare bones of the thought and picture I want to convey. It's not about trying to sound fancy.

LSM: I want to ask you more about your beginnings as a writer. Have you written continually from the time you dictated your first poems to your mother?

KK: There was a gap of several years between my early childhood interest in writing and my junior high and high school years, when I wrote a great deal of poetry. By then, I was reading *The Waste Land*. I also recall writing a school paper in which I made the case for e. e. cummings as a "serious" poet.

LSM: How did your first children's book, *Roar and More,* come about?

KK: As an undergraduate, I transferred from Antioch to the Yale University School of Art, thinking that I would eventually have a career in commercial art. At Yale, I studied graphic design, and when we were given the assignment of designing and printing a book, I produced a children's picture book called *Roar and More,* for which I made linoleum block cuts, wrote a series of verses, and set the type. As part of the project I also wrote a paper on the history of children's books. So I already had an interest in the field. After college, when I went out looking for a job, *Roar and More* was in my portfolio, but I was really looking for work as a designer. My first job was as assistant to a fashion photographer. Then I worked as an assistant in the graphic arts department at *Industrial Design* magazine. But I soon found that I did not like working for other people. For one thing, I couldn't take naps, which I like to do. And I didn't like having people boss me around. So when I had my first book published, and then a second book, I quit. When I first went to Harper's I was going to see about a freelance jacket assignment for the adult trade department. But for various reasons I ended up meeting with the children's book department, too, and so, in a sense, my career in children's books began by chance.

LSM: At what point did you begin to think of yourself as a children's book author and artist rather than as a graphic designer who made picture books, as it were, on the side?

KK: I remember that some time early on in my career, Father, who hated working in advertising and was a good writer, asked me, "Are you going to do children's books all your life?" What he meant was, "Where's the novel?" I felt hurt. Yet I probably also agreed with him at the time that I should write for grown-ups. Children's books were becoming my work, however, the thing I knew how to do.

I have a very beautifully calligraphed sign that my father gave me, which reads: "Anything worth doing is worth doing for money." It was important to me when I got out of school to know I could make a living. I felt this way in part because my mother, who had come to New York to become an actress, and after a brief stage career had become a professional photographer, stopped working altogether after I was born, and I knew she regretted it. I grew up determined that I would not let this happen to me, that I would be able to work and have a family. In children's books, I found a way of doing this. Many of my women friends postponed their careers until after their children were older. I did not want to wait.

LSM: Had you written much poetry in the years leading up to the time that you published *In the Middle of the Trees* (1958)?

KK: My oeuvre was not extensive. But I had written verse in high school and in college, including the text for *Roar and More.* When I met Harper's editor Ursula Nordstrom, she asked me what else I had to show her, and so I presented her with a sheaf of typed poetry. When I got the poems back, I found on the top of some pages, in Ursula's handwriting, B+, C–, and so on. Ursula had graded my work. The B's and C's did not make it into my book.

LSM: That was a witty thing for her to have done, but there was also an edge to it, especially considering that you were the Yalie just out of school.

KK: It was very witty—and it almost finished me off. Ursula, of course, could be very funny. Part of our relationship consisted of being funny with each other.

LSM: Was writing your second book hard for you, as it is for so many writers?

KK: I married a musician just after graduation, had my first book contract, and thought, what do I do for an encore? That first post-school summer my husband and I were given the use of a Quonset hut on Cape Cod for a week. Charlie would be in the Quonset hut playing the oboe. He used to say that an oboe has a sound that cuts through cement. Well, it can also cut through a Quonset hut. It rained all week. The rain beat down on the tin roof like a drum. With all that noise to contend with, I took my Royal portable typewriter and sat in the car hoping to work. I had one verse in my head: "In winter when the snow is deep / The black-haired bears fall fast asleep." I also had the story that went with the lines. It was going to be about a child going out on a snowy winter's day, asking various animals he meets, "What do you do when it snows?" As I sat in the car with my typewriter in my lap, the snow turned into rain, and my first lines became: "James pressed his nose against the pane / And saw a million drops of rain . . ." In *James and the Rain* (1957), which was my second book, James then goes out and asks the animals what they do in the rain.

LSM: Did becoming a parent greatly influence your work?

KK: My son Nick was born in 1960. By then I had done four or five books. I got to the point where I could draw with a child sitting on my lap. I found that I loved having things going on around me—

even if my mother-in-law and others didn't believe that I could possibly be doing real work if I was working at home.

When I was pregnant with Nick, I went back to the lines "In winter when the snow is deep . . . etc.," and used it in *The Bear Who Saw the Spring* (1961). In that story, a bear takes a puppy around, showing him the changes in nature that take place in the course of a year. In writing that story, I suppose I was really trying to imagine myself showing the world to my son.

L S M : *The Philharmonic Gets Dressed* is not written in verse, but the text has some of the qualities of poetry, does it not?

K K : It does for me, as does the text of *Jerusalem, Shining Still* (1987). In both books, the writing entailed a process of chiseling away—trying to get each sentence as simple and rhythmic and right in its context as possible. Even a joke has to be told with just the right rhythm; otherwise it's going to limp away, and the humor will be lost. I don't think I ever considered writing *The Philharmonic Gets Dressed* in verse, but I did try that for another book of mine, called *Just Like Everyone Else* (1959), but I found it was not working. The story of that book is a simple children's joke. Verse wasn't right for it because, as I eventually realized, it had to be told with a poker face, and the driving rhythm of the verse broke the mood and became intrusive. But to go back to *The Philharmonic*. I rewrote the text over and over again, reading it out loud as I worked, as I always do.

L S M : Tell me more about how *The Philharmonic Gets Dressed* evolved.

K K : I had started by writing about one musician. Later, I realized the book would be funnier and look great if it was about the whole orchestra.

I knew that children want to understand how things work. They want specifics. I remembered that when I was given a new doll as a

Karla Kuskin •

child, the first thing I always did was to look to see what was under the skirt—what was really going on. Long before *The Philharmonic*, I had mentioned underwear in a poem called "A Bug Sat in a Silver Flower" in my collection *Near the Window Tree*, and I always got a big laugh when I read that poem to seven- and eight- and nine-year-olds. So for that reason, too, I knew that kids would be intrigued by a story about grown-ups putting on their own clothes, about music and underwear.

LSM: I don't suppose you had to do research for that book.

KK: Yes, I did. In the text I say, for instance, how many women and how many men there are in the orchestra, and I wanted to be accurate about the percentages. I also checked to make sure I had the musicians' clothes just right and that I didn't have musicians carrying instruments out onto the stage that in reality would have been set up on stage ahead of time.

LSM: Did the text change once Marc Simont went to work on the illustrations?

KK: No, it stayed pretty much the same. Marc was my choice to illustrate the book as well as my editor's. He did a wonderful job, and I would say that the words and pictures of *The Philharmonic Gets Dressed* come as close to expressing a single unified idea as a picture book can.

LSM: You seem not to like to repeat yourself. What, then, was it like to plan and then write your sequel to *The Philharmonic Gets Dressed*, called *The Dallas Titans Get Ready for Bed* (1986)?

KK: I don't like to repeat myself. You're right. But everybody loved *The Philharmonic*, and people kept saying, "Why don't you do one like this?" and "Why don't you do one like that?" I even started writing a book about Attila the Hun having lunch as he went about his conquests. The details were about what he had for lunch. I had a lot of far-fetched ideas. That one was a little too sophisticated for children. Then I thought of writing about a sports team, and at first it was going to be a baseball team because baseball was a sport I knew something about. The problem was that baseball players don't wear interesting clothes. But football players—I've always hated football—look so funny to me. They walk out onto the field with all that gear on, and then they fall down. They get up, and then they fall down again. I know that that is terrible to say. But it was a good idea for a book, and so I got several advisors, including a sports writer who was very helpful, and my stepdaughter helped, and others. Then I had a terrible time finding the right title because the name of the team had to sound real without, for legal reasons, being an actual team name. When I wrote the text, I kept in mind the voices of children who don't want to go to bed. *The Dallas Titans*, I think, is more about playing a game, whereas *The Philharmonic* is more about art. In *The Philharmonic*, that is, I tried to show that making art—or doing anything creative—is real work, and that that means having to get up and get washed and dressed and practice and show up on time and not be off-key.

LSM: A moment ago, you suggested a stylistic link between *The Philharmonic Gets Dressed* and *Jerusalem, Shining Still*. Would you say more about the connection you see between those two books?

KK: One day I received a phone call from a woman who was representing the office of Teddy Kollek, then the mayor of Jerusalem. This woman said that she admired *The Philharmonic Gets Dressed* and wondered whether I would be interested in coming to Jerusalem and writing a book for children based on what I had learned about the city. She thought I might be able to see Jerusalem through the lens, so to speak, of *The Philharmonic Gets Dressed*—a city where a lot of different people live and work together. So I went to Israel and for three weeks lived in the government's official guest house in Jerusalem, with a view of Mount Zion. Each day I would visit museums or talk with experts of various kinds. There are great advantages to being a stranger because as a stranger you pay attention to everything, and that's what children do. And that is also what you want to do as a writer or as an artist drawing: to see what is different and what is important. For me, the story of Jerusalem was the story of its survival through centuries of batterings and burnings and wars. I decided I wanted to write that history for children—four thousand years on the head of a pin. It had to be very compact and so, as with *The Philharmonic*, the writing became a process of cutting and searching for the right rhythms, the right words. There were so many names to reckon with that I tried to make a song of them, a kind of repeating and growing chorus, with each new conqueror added to the list. I wanted the reader to come out not necessarily remembering all the names but knowing some of what the city survived.

LSM: I want to return now to the subject of poetry. How would you say that poetry for children has fared lately?

KK: When Ursula Nordstrom published my first book of poems, *In the Middle of the Trees*, in 1958, there weren't many other people writing poetry collections for children. Now it's a field. What hasn't fared well, however, is children's books. Poetry in particular needs to stay in print in order to be reread, savored, and passed on by word of mouth. But most poetry doesn't sell wonderfully well, and only major sellers are staying in print.

LSM: Children today hear so many catchy phrases and advertising jingles in the media. How does poetry fit into that world? Can a poem, for instance, provide children with relief from the frenzy and sheer noise the media generate? Or does poetry simply get drowned out?

KK: I can remember as a child that at night, on days when we had gone to the movies, I would lie in bed, close my eyes, and, starting with the first frame, try to replay the whole movie in my head. Movies today jump around so rapidly that this would be impossible to do. Television and movies fragment thought, particularly narrative thought. Everything has become chopped up, and our sense of time has become distorted and malleable. It is very hard under these conditions to tell a story with a beginning, a middle, and an end succesfully. Not many writers today know how to do it. But the kind of poetry we have been talking about fits in very nicely with contemporary media. Poetry can deal with discontinuity. It can jump around, give you a short take. It doesn't have to sustain a narrative.

And poetry has other powers, too. A poem reins you into its rhythms. It slows you down and makes you listen to words. I remember a grammar-school teacher saying, "Now put your heads down on your desks. I'm going to read to you." Then she would say, "Close your eyes. Relax. Just think of the pictures these words make." That kind of listening can be very compelling.

LSM: You make the experience of listening to a poem sound like the experience of listening to the radio.

KK: I think it is. Poems are more like radio than television. They are perhaps also more like drawings than paintings. They give us word pictures akin to illustrations: the translation into words of an image or perhaps of a very short fantasy.

LSM: Are poems more like drawings than paintings because so much is left out?

KK: Not quite: it's because what is left out is so important, as important as what remains.

....

James Marshall

Born October 10, 1942
San Antonio, Texas
Died October 13, 1992
New York, New York

....

As a writer, James Marshall specialized in sly comic tales highlighting life's little surprises—friendship's complications or the consequences of biting off more than one can chew. As an illustrator, he favored drawings sporting a look of devil-may-care abandon, a quicksilver effect he was generally prepared, as he liked to say, to "sweat bullets" to achieve. As Maurice Sendak has recalled, Marshall was, in fact, "a perfectionist in all things." With the publication of George and Martha (1972), the first of many picture books he both wrote and illustrated, he established himself as a master of tongue-in-cheek understatement, true-to-type characterization, and dead-on comic timing. During a prolific career, Marshall created (at times in collaboration with the writer Harry Allard) a parade of freshly imagined, over-the-top characters: Fox, the Cut-Ups, Miss Nelson, Viola Swamp, and the Stupids, among others. Marshall heroes come out all right in the end, but just by the seat of their pants.

Marshall himself was a compulsively funny, extravagant man who wore his vulnerabilities on his sleeve. While accepting slapstick and light satire as his natural modes of expression, he regretted the lack of serious attention these tendencies all but guaranteed his creative efforts. "Zany,"

Marshall once said, "[is] a word I'd like to have wiped off every dust jacket of every book I've ever done."

Marshall's retelling of Goldilocks and the Three Bears *(1988) garnered the artist his first major award, a Caldecott Honor, in 1989. This interview was recorded in Marshall's New York apartment on May 24 of that year.*

LEONARD S. MARCUS: Tell me about your first memories of books. Do you remember learning to read?

JAMES MARSHALL: No, I can't remember that, but I do remember a few of the first books I knew, including *Tubby the Tugboat* and *The Little Engine That Could.* My mother, who is a great reader, had a Palmer Cox's *Brownies* book. I can still sort of smell it. In fact, I still have it somewhere. Very early on, I started reading adult books. My favorite when I was six was Stefan Zweig's *Marie Antoinette.* I don't know if I could read, but I got very interested, and then my mother gave me Charles Dickens' *A Child's History of England.* So that's the sort of thing I read, or pretended I was reading. I think I learned to read by osmosis.

LSM: What other kinds of reading matter did you have at home?

JM: Mostly my mother's old movie magazines from the twenties. I may, in fact, have learned to read from *Silver Screen.* She was a great movie nut, who saw every new picture. I didn't start paying attention to kids' books until I was in my mid-twenties. Maurice [Sendak]'s *Where the Wild Things Are* and a fabulous book by Domenico Gnoli called *The Art of Smiling*, which was also published in the sixties, got me started. Like a fool I looked at those two picture books and said, "Well I can do that." And so I started drawing.

LSM: You hadn't drawn much as a child?

JM: Probably not—just the way kids doodle when they're kids.

There was a time when I was passionately interested in drawing, but then I quit, absolutely quit. I was ten or eleven. My father had decided that I would be a musician. That was what I was going to be. One day he brought home a violin, and I started playing. I was aimed to be a musician. After that, I went to music school and spent summers at the Interlocken, Michigan, music camp. In high school I realized I would need a college scholarship, and that I would have a better chance as a viola student than as a violinist, because violinists were in much better supply in the fifties. So I switched over to the viola and got scholarships everywhere. I could pick and choose, and I chose to go to the New England Conservatory in Boston.

LSM: Earlier on, while you were still living in Texas with your parents, were you known among your classmates as the school musician?

JM: I was the school creep! A couple of my creepy friends and I were the artists of Beaumont High School. I love my hometown, San Antonio. But my father, who worked for Southern Pacific Railroad, was transferred to Beaumont when I was in high school, and I did not like Beaumont nearly as well. Beaumont is below sea level. It's a swamp. And there I was, arriving in the ninth grade, not knowing anybody—and playing the violin. I knew I had to get out of there, and a scholarship was the only way. So I practiced fiendishly!

LSM: Does the name Viola Swamp owe anything to your feelings about Beaumont?

JM: Yes, exactly. It's the two put together. When Harry Allard and I do books together we generally can't say who wrote what. But that one—she's mine! I think she's my favorite character, actually.

LSM: If you practiced so diligently, you can't have been much of a cutup.

JM: I wasn't a cutup, but I was a smart-ass kid. I was always trying to show off in school by getting good grades and so on. But I didn't have the courage to be a real brat.

LSM: So you think of the Cut-Ups as being brave?

JM: In a way. I was very timid. I was a coward. I remember once when a kid fell and slashed his forehead badly, I ran the other way. I didn't help him. For years I was tortured with that. The Cut-Ups are just kids I know in my neighborhood in Connecticut. They're either going to end up doing time or. . . . I think they're both geniuses. One of them is now becoming a little actor in local plays and summer stock, so I think he's going to be okay. But they're not me at all. I loved school. I was crazy about school.

LSM: The Alamo is in San Antonio.

JM: I was born across the street from the Alamo!

LSM: Was it exciting for you to be growing up in a place with such a rich history?

JM: Actually, I grew up out in the country, twenty miles out of town. So I really grew up alone. I had no friends after school. We lived in San Antonio after I was about twelve. My baby sister was born there. But earlier on I lived out on that farm. I think that's where all the imagination came from. I was passionately interested in English history, so I imagined the back forty as the site of the Battle of Bosworth Field. I had no sense of its being Texas. It was always someplace else.

LSM: Texas wasn't historical enough, so to speak?

JM: That's how it seemed for a time. But then I got very interested in my father's family, all of whom were from West Texas, and became passionately interested in the West. In the 1880s when they settled in West Texas they were still having Indian raids. At one point—this was about 1910—Poncho Villa raided my grandmother's ranch and stole her cattle. As a ten-year-old hearing that stuff—my imagination went wild.

LSM: Were there good storytellers in your family?

JM: My grandfather, for one. I would pump him and the others for information. Once I discovered boxes and boxes of Brownie pictures, and I asked my grandmother about them and she said, "Hon, out here that was all we could do." It was flat for miles, with nothing going on. So when they got their Brownies, they took pictures of each other constantly. I found photographs of my grandparents in buckboards, with shotguns. It was the end of the frontier era, and I had certifiable proof that my family had lived through it. That seemed just wonderful to me.

LSM: Do you still have those photographs?

JM: I have many of them. I always come back from Texas with some album that nobody wants.

LSM: There are Texas flags in the schoolrooms in your books. Is that because you are still fond of the state?

JM: Yes. Really, my roots are there. I like the climate. I'm especially fond of West Texas. I went to bury my grandmother two years ago in a little town called Marathon, named after Marathon in Greece. It's like a ghost town. There's nothing there, except for a windmill. And when I arrived in town I noticed that the windmill—I always put windmills in my books, too—was being taken down. I said, "You can't do that." It was the only thing there. It was like the Eiffel Tower of Marathon, Texas. So they said, "Well, if you want it, you buy it." So I bought it. Now I own a windmill in the middle of God-knows-where. I bought it with the stipulation that it stays—you know—on Grandma's grave! She had a fairly good sense of humor and was a pretty good storyteller herself.

LSM: Was coming east to study in Boston a turning point in your life?

JM: Yes. I knew that I had to get out of Beaumont, and I wanted to come east. Someone said that Boston was the place to go.

LSM: Had you been studying languages by then? I know that at some point you studied French and Italian. Both languages are so musical, and I wonder if the musical connection was part of their appeal for you?

JM: No. It was snobbery. I have always gone into things from the wrong end, the superficial end. I think I became an artist because I wanted a studio, because I wanted to buy art supplies! Then came the time when I had to prove something. I always wanted to love opera, symphonies, classical music—to distinguish myself. Later, I realized I really like these things. I'm not alone in this. I know a lot of people who say they were little snobs at fifteen, then suddenly it took.

LSM: I have read that while you were in music school you were in a plane crash and injured your hand.

JM: I don't know why I said that. It's not true. I was in a slight accident that had nothing to do with a plane, and I did injure my hand. I suppose I decided to make a good story out of it. But I did botch up my hand and got a condition of permanently inflamed muscles. I would practice, and it would only get worse and worse. At the age of eighteen I had to stop playing. Suddenly, I had no career, no future—nothing. It was a horrible, horrible time.

And so I had to go back to Beaumont, and with little towns like that, when you go back you never get out again. But by the grace of God, my father was transferred back to San Antonio. This was when I was eighteen or nineteen and had had one year of the Conservatory. So I went back to Beaumont for about a year and enrolled in Lamar State College of Technology, where of all people Janis Joplin was a fellow student. I was a year older than Janis. I don't know how many times I changed my major. But that was how I got out of Beaumont the second time. After Lamar State, I went back to school in the East, and then taught high school in Boston, which nearly killed me because I was teaching Spanish, and I didn't speak a word of the language. It was very odd.

LSM: How did you manage it?

JM: I also lacked teaching credentials, which meant that I couldn't teach in the public schools. But I knew I still might be able to teach at a private school, and I did have a degree in French. So I called up a certain Mother Superior about a job, and her first question was, "Do you speak Spanish?" When I replied, "I spent two weeks in Mexico City once," she said, "Come right over!" If that wasn't bad enough—because you can always intimidate high school students—half the kids in that school were Puerto Rican. I was really in a jam—so I blackmailed them. I said, "If you give me trouble, you'll never get into another Catholic school in the world." I'm not even a Catholic, but that's what I said. Their little eyes popped out. I said, "If you shut up, I'll give you a C. If you teach me some Spanish, I'll give you a B." So we worked this out as best we could. They were very impressed. I got through two years of that. I did teach the kids some French. But I quickly realized that I would die of a stroke if I had to teach high school for the rest of my life. That's when I started drawing. That's when the doodling began.

LSM: As an escape?

JM: Yes. Have you ever taught high school? You're constantly on, from eight in the morning until three. You get so few breaks you're just about dead by the end of the day. I feel so sorry for school-teachers. They somehow have to have more stamina than the rest of us. I think they become like cockroaches—after a certain point, NOTHING CAN DESTROY THEM. I knew I had to do something else. I would come home and draw late at night. And a friend of mine who was an editor at Houghton Mifflin said, "This is children's book art." By then I sort of was trying to do children's book art because I had seen *Where the Wild Things Are* and Gnoli's book and the work of Tomi Ungerer. And I was crazy about Edward Gorey's stuff. And then I saw Arnold Lobel's *Frog and Toad* books with their very short chapters. I thought, I can do that. God only knows how I did it. Doing two- or three-page stories is the hardest thing. I think I also got into doing children's books because I thought it would be easy. It's a lot of fun sometimes—but it ain't easy. That's basically how I got started. I brought in my portfolio on napkins and things to Walter Lorraine. It was all very nice. He called back the next day and said, "We have a book for you to illustrate." It was Byrd Baylor's *Plink, Plink, Plink* (1971). And so I was off and running.

LSM: Going back for a moment to your teaching days. Despite the difficulties, did you empathize with your students on some level? Did getting to know them take you back to childhood or teenage feelings of your own?

JM: I liked the kids a lot. They were rotten kids, a lot of them, and very hard to discipline. I was teaching in the South End. Some of the kids had never been to downtown Boston. I became very, very fond of them. Oddly enough, it was when I learned to discipline them, to shut them up—it's that paradox: you can't be their pals—that I became very fond of them. And I find I'm very fond of kids now.

LSM: Given the circumstances you described earlier, did you really think of yourself as a teacher?

JM: It was complete role-playing. I knew that a lot of it was very false. I think you have to act and role-play when you're sitting at the drawing board, too. You have to play the role of the artist at least long enough to get yourself to the drawing board, and then you get caught up in that wonderful trance and you forget yourself. I think the one thing that disturbed me the most about teaching was the fatigue. I don't know how good a teacher I was. It was the same, later, at the Parsons School of Design, where I took over Maurice's picture book class and was accused of great favoritism. The problem was that there were two geniuses in the class, and I would spend all

James Marshall

my time with them. I was very inspired by them, and I didn't pay any attention to the others, which I guess was not fair. So I gave up teaching. Teaching is fun, but you have to be very careful about what you're doing.

I did at least teach them all what a picture book is—that no matter what the style, there are certain principles that underlie the picture book as a genre. How to move it. When to stop it. How to pace it. What to leave out. All sorts of little tricks. Never to have the action going into the gutter. A picture book becomes a whole world if it's done properly. I'm very surprised that sometimes people don't understand this, or realize that the picture book is a true art form.

LSM: When you were doodling on napkins, were you already creating animal characters like George and Martha?

JM: Yes, but not George and Martha. They came along a little later. I quit teaching even before I got the job illustrating Byrd Baylor's book, having decided I was going to make it in publishing—or at least to try to. Then I went home to Texas for a while. I was still living there when I started developing George and Martha in a sketchbook.

LSM: So one day you just hit upon the idea of hippopotamuses as characters?

JM: Somebody else told me they were hippos. I started out with two little dots on the page. They were imperfections in the paper. That's how I got started. And my mother was watching *Who's Afraid of Virginia Woolf?* on television. That was my inspiration for George and Martha's names. I usually don't tell kiddies that. I once was on a live radio show in Chicago, and when I arrived at the station I asked the woman, "Do you need any information about me?" "No," she said, "I've done my homework." We went on the air, and suddenly she wants to know, "What's it like writing about the First

Family?" So I say, "Well, it's not that George and Martha!" "Who are they, then?" "Well . . . they're hippos." From that moment on, she was completely lost! I had to take over.

LSM: So you had those two dots to begin with, and the characters somehow emerged from them. The stories are so wonderfully compact. Did you try to write several stories at once in order to find out more about your new characters?

JM: First I drew them in various situations. Out of a scene would come a story. The fun of writing, of course, is paring the story down, whittling it down to the right word. You can become so self-conscious, so precious. You have to be careful not to get too sculptured. If I've got a character that I'm interested in, I can trust that I'll soon have a story as well. The story comes from the character. The ending is always my problem. I've ruined so many books with not-good endings. I find that when you read a book or see a movie, that if fabulous, wonderful things have gone on, and if the ending doesn't give that period to it, you come out or close the book feeling you've seen or read something second-rate. I'm always so grateful when I know what the ending will be.

LSM: What is your idea of a good ending?

JM: A good ending is inevitable but it's also a surprise.

LSM: George and Martha get into little moral dilemmas from time to time, yet the stories don't feel moralistic.

JM: God, I hope not. But I think that when there is a moral dilemma, I'm usually doing it tongue-in-cheek. If there's "teaching," it comes out of their characters and not little sayings or whatever. For instance, "Always tell your friends the truth" is a great lie, and you wouldn't always do that.

LSM: When George and Martha disagree, there is usually some merit in both their points of view.

JM: I hope it isn't self-conscious. Sometimes I'm afraid it is. The situation has to be there. It has to be organic. If you try to impose a little moral, it gets very sticky.

LSM: How would you describe George and Martha?

JM: I think innocent, crafty, courtly. They're very courtly with each other. They usually have exquisite manners in the best sense. I think they have a sense of fun. I had a dream about Martha. She had become very cross with me. She wanted better stories, better lines. And I distinctly remember her telling me that if she didn't get them she was going to Maurice's house. I woke up in a cold sweat!

One of my favorite authors is Chekhov, and one of the reasons I love his stories and plays so much is that things are not spelled out in them. It's in the story, it's in the characters, it's in the setting, and it's all very intuitive. You don't have to dot the *i*'s. At the same time, you've got to have a sense of artifice, too. Because it's the real world filtered through one intelligence and point of view.

LSM: Your *George and Martha* drawings are very elegant, yet there's also something artless about them.

JM: Maurice said they were "raw." They have to be fresh, and the line has to be alive. Sometimes it takes a long time to achieve that quality. At other times I can just do it.

LSM: When you say that the line has to be alive, what exactly do you mean?

JM: It has to tell a story. It has to be an interpretation of something. It's there for a meaning rather than for an absolute realistic reflection.

LSM: In Edward Lear's drawings, there's an obsessive, crazily manic quality to the line that certainly suits his subject matter. Can you describe your line in comparable terms? In the *George and Martha* books, for instance, are you trying for a "heavy" line to emphasize the characters' massive physique?

JM: It's heavy but my hand shakes a little when I do it. I do it in pencil and then I trace. Sometimes I do a basic pencil drawing to establish an architecture for the drawing. I really cannot stand it if something in a picture is misplaced. Scale is very important. I think I learned a lot about scale from looking at Maurice's work, although he and I don't approach scale in the same way. For me, it is like focusing in and out. There is only one point where that character should be in relation to the frame and to the viewer and to the back wall, and I spend hours erasing, pulling it down, bringing it up, until it's absolutely perfect, the way I want it. And then I have to forget all of that and make the line come alive for the finished drawing. So often the line gets tight, and when I look at a drawing the next morning, I say, "This has got to go out. It doesn't have that spontaneous quality."

Edward Gorey's work has enormous thought behind it. Someone said once that Gorey has been doing the same book for twenty or thirty years. It's not true. He keeps perfecting, getting better and better. We all have bad books every so often. I think that when you have a highly recognizable style it can read to some people as formula. It can, of course, become formula, too, and that's one of the worst things that can happen to an artist. I don't know how someone in that situation could stand himself.

LSM: George and Martha are quite vulnerable in many ways. Would you relate the shakiness of the line to that quality of theirs?

JM: No, I think the shakiness is just to keep it from becoming too tight. It's a technique, although anything you do on the page relates to psychology. They are vulnerable, and I think that's why kids, at least, like them. And because they're not fools. My characters usually have their wits about them. And they have the gift of wit, which can be a saving grace. How many of us have gotten out of awful situations by falling back on our sense of humor?

James Marshall

LSM: How do you see George and Martha in relation to each other?

JM: They probably reflect two sides of my own personality. He bumbles into things through innocence, I think, and she gets a little grand in places. It's so silly that these light little entertainments can spark people, but I've gotten outraged letters. I got one recently from a Presbyterian minister in Tennessee who was just furious with me! He said, first of all, I was clearly a woman writing under a man's name, that I was a rabid feminist because the female character was always dominating the male character; and, second of all, that he had been to Africa and had heard that hippos kill people. How dare I! I thought, oh God, this might be the one letter I answer back! Then I thought, that's not really me. Martha's really quite pretentious in many ways.

LSM: When you put together a *George and Martha* book, do you think a great deal about the ordering of the stories? Is there an emotional arc or contour to their arrangement?

JM: Very definitely. You've got to think about what that second story's going to be. It's very important. It's just the same with pacing any kind of book. When to let up. When to turn up the juice. When to give a rest. When not to betray the characters. And always doing something that is within the context of their lives and personalities. There are so many considerations.

LSM: Did your musical training carry over into your children's book work in any way?

JM: It's very funny. I have some tapes of myself playing the viola— I was pretty good, actually—and I think the way I approached playing the viola is very much the way I approach drawing now. There is some correlation between sound and space. I don't understand it. But I know that as a violist I had a very fat sound. I can almost say that the musical line I created when I played the viola is the line with which I now draw. It has the same weight. The viola is the alto voice of the string family. That's the sort of tonality of my drawings. It sounds so pretentious to say it, but I know it's true.

LSM: There's a clarity to your drawings that relates to what you said earlier about leaving things out. Do your drawings get less cluttered as you work on them?

JM: Oh, yes. It's one of my major concerns. Concerns—but not problems. Speaking broadly, I almost never have major problems, or a crack-up, doing a drawing. I draw with a lot of confidence. I don't know if it's going to be a good drawing or not, but it's going to be what I want. The real hell is constructing a plot, doing the *Miss Nelson* books, for instance, and getting the story to finally come together in that satisfying way. I sometimes do a book in a few weeks. Other times it may take a year. If I have one book that's successful, I may sign a contract for a sequel. I've got the character, so I'm confident about that. But then I think, how did I get into this? I'm going to go crazy! This is awful! Then I start drawing, and the solution comes out of that, and I say "Ah!" I don't know where I'd be if I didn't know how to draw.

LSM: I like the half-title pages in the *George and Martha* books. They remind me of the titles in old-fashioned newsreels and silent pictures.

JM: I have always thought of them as a way of introducing kids to books—books with chapters and chapter headings. And with a this-little-story-will-only-take-you-three-pages-to-get-through kind of feeling.

I have drawers and drawers of *George and Martha* stories. Some are finished, others not. I have always wanted to do a book—and I may do one—as a sort of scrapbook, or sketchbook with bits of stories—maybe even a sort of funny, juiced-up workbook for kids. I have the beginnings, I guess, of a hundred stories that never went anywhere, which I know somebody could finish. I have one picture of cows dancing a tango-y dance, and the caption reads, "From the day the Hoovers learned they could dance, their lives have never been the same." Then you turn the page and—NOTHING. I have lots of stories like that. Then I have middles of stories, and I think it might be fun just to put eight of them together and say, "Take it, kids—and send me the royalties!"

I have always thought my best stuff was in my sketchbooks. I have hundreds and hundreds of sketchbooks. I like to work at night, I suppose because that's when my defenses are sort of low. I have my most creative ideas at night. I'm less inhibited, and I really let it rip.

LSM: Going back to George and Martha. Unlike Albee's *Who's Afraid of Virginia Woolf?*, your books present the world as a fundamentally gentle and hospitable place.

JM: Maybe I'm just hoping it's an OK place. Somebody said to me on television in San Francisco that the books are very sunny. Maybe I hope the world is full of innocence. But this woman asked me the same question. She said, "You must have a sunny, happy, healthy outlook on the world." And I said, "Well, let me think about it. I think most people are selfish and venal, and that we deserve the horrors that have come into the world." She looked at me as if she had this snake sitting across from her—a snake who writes *George and Martha* books! I think to do a sunny, happy book doesn't necessarily mean that you're a sunny, happy person.

LSM: I wasn't suggesting the books are sentimental.

JM: I don't mind being light. Max Beerbohm said that there are many charming talents that ruin themselves by taking themselves too seriously.

LSM: In the *George and Martha* books, you nonetheless also show that life is always a little more complicated than one thought.

JM: If that has come across, I'm delighted. I think that is how I do feel. At the same time, just doing a well-made book is in a way profound, too. It gives people a great sense of well-being to look at a book that is put together well and that operates on the level it set out to do. That alone—just to be able to do that—is an achievement. I'm often asked what's my favorite book, and I say I don't know because I haven't been able to do it yet.

But there are pages, and sometimes series of pages, where I feel I've got it right. The entrances of Viola Swamp, I think, are particularly successful. She is sort of Maria Callas with a fake nose on. "Here I am!" *Crash.* And I think *Red Riding Hood* (1987) was successful. Then again, it's happened to me a lot that I'll think, Ah, I've really got something here. People are going to sit up and take notice, fall on the floor laughing. And the next morning I think, I ought to be hospitalized. This is terrible! Often I've been surprised that stuff that was sheer drudgery—you know, you just feel nausea in every cell of your body—but then the book gets published and it's this light, fluffy piece that works, with some humor in it. And you think, Where the hell did that come from?

LSM: George and Martha look more like adults than children. But it's not clear how old they are.

JM: I think that's good. I must do it deliberately. They're not children. It's clear they're not kids. It's also not so clear that they're grown-ups. And I find it interesting when people ask, "Are they ever going to get married?" Things like that. Because that would never occur to me. "Childlike" and "innocent"—I wonder if they're the same? You never know how they make their money. You never know anything realistic about them. Their houses are as goofy as can be, yet I don't think they're cardboard cutouts. There is some dimension to them.

LSM: You like to play with the margins. Often a character will step halfway off the page.

JM: I got criticized for that somewhere. Obviously, it's something that I do deliberately. I've always loved Japanese prints, and anybody who is influenced by Japanese prints will start doing that sort of thing. It's a technique, and it does wonderful things dramatically.

LSM: Do you think of the page of a book as a sort of proscenium stage?

JM: Sure. I don't think of it as a cartoon strip. Many times my stuff has been called "cartoony." I think that's just wrong. I think of books as theater. I love the opera. I love the theater. The more artificial the better. The more artificial it is, if it is well done, the truer it is.

LSM: By "artificial" do you mean the more it calls attention to itself as a book?

JM: Oftentimes I love backstage more than what's up front. But that's just a quirk. I do think of the page as a proscenium.

LSM: George and Martha are always changing costumes. Part of the fun of those books is in seeing what they'll have on next. That in itself makes them a little like actors.

JM: I'm beginning to like them all over again! I might do another.

LSM: Why did you invent a "collaborator" for yourself named Edward Marshall?

JM: Walter Lorraine at Houghton Mifflin absolutely killed me at one point because I had published under the name Edward Marshall with another publisher, Dial. But Houghton didn't do easy-to-read books, and Phyllis Fogelman at Dial did. So that was the beginning of Edward. One day somebody called me after I'd come back from a long publishing lunch—I was really quite tipsy—and said, "Mr. Marshall?" I said, "Yeeessss . . ." "Can you tell us where we can find Edward Marshall?" And I said, "Well, he's very difficult to find . . . living out there by the crematorium, with those fourteen children." I could hear his pencil scratching away! I made up this incredible tale—and it was published, I forget where. You know, "The Biography of Edward Marshall." But then finally Walter figured out that there was no Edward Marshall—my middle name is Edward—and Phyllis and I decided that it would be better for the reviews of the *Fox* books to appear under "James." So we were having lunch in midtown, and Phyllis was saying, "Well, you know, I think he should die in a hang-gliding accident off Carmel." And I said, "No, Phyllis . . ." And I noticed these two at the next table looking VERY interested in our conversation. I think Edward just sort of faded away.

LSM: What about Harry Allard? Does he exist?

JM: Yes, UNFORTUNATELY. Actually he's a very good friend of mine. He lives in Mexico and is the one who taught me French. We've done the *Stupids* books and the *Miss Nelson* books and a few others. Collaboration is not a lot of fun. But Harry has a wonderful sense of humor. He invented the Stupids. You can imagine the kinds of letters we get about that series. "How dare you make fun of the mentally deficient?" "Oh, I've been trying to keep children from using the word *stupid* all my life . . ." People are just outraged.

I suspect that most adults who object to those books—nine times out of ten—have not looked at them with children. I find that the kids who read the books don't think the stories are stupid at all. They think maybe the jerk who wrote them is stupid because there's a cow on the wall. And I've noticed that when kids are first starting to read, and the word *doesn't* correspond to whatever the picture is, they find it screamingly funny.

LSM: There again, it's showing that the world is a little more complicated than one thought, isn't it? Instead of words and pictures matching up, there are reversals of sense.

JM: I think that runs all through my work, in a sort of benign way. The Stupids, for instance, always have a good time.

LSM: They don't know enough not to.

JM: Right. They have a certain joie de vivre. They're fun to do in part because the level of humor is right on the edge of stupidity itself.

LSM: Do you do many school visits?

JM: I used to. I quit because it was taking too much time. I loved it, though. It was terrifying at first, mainly I think because having gone through three years as a substitute teacher in ghetto schools (that was before I taught high school), and not having been able to discipline the kids, I was really scared to death of them. But I always loved grammar school, and once I got back into that atmosphere, I gave a sigh. I just loved it. And the kids—I was thunderstruck that I had a rapport with them. At first I thought, I'm pulling the wool over these kids' eyes. I was very surprised that they really liked me. They got the jokes. Fourth graders are the ones for me. Third and fourth graders. They can really scream with laughter because they have a little bit of sophistication. I think they catch on.

LSM: Would you draw pictures for them?

JM: Well, see, I can draw like the wind so they would shut up immediately. That conquered the discipline problem right from the start. Their little eyes would pop out of their heads, so long as they could see. Some of these God-awful principals, on the other hand . . . I'd say, "A group of sixty is all I can handle"—and then suddenly I'd be shown into the auditorium or the cafeteria where six hundred kids would file in. None of them can see. It's overheated. The teachers want a free hour. That's vaudeville hell—with the audience squirming and your voice just going.

LSM: Is it true that kids would sometimes ask you about *George and Martha* stories that aren't in any of the books?

JM: Yes. They write their own stories, of course. But often I'd have kids tell me things that they thought were in the books, that weren't. We all do that to some extent, since we can't read the author's mind and must interpret every word of a book in our own way. But I think anybody who does the kind of open-ended book that I do must have similar experiences with readers.

LSM: Can you think of an example of a story that some child imagined reading in one of your books?

JM: "When Martha Sank Her Boat" is one of them. I thought at first, Well, I've forgotten about that one. I'd better go back and look. Well, I did, and there's nothing about Martha sinking a boat. There's another one about George blowing up Martha with dynamite. I thought, I'd better speak to the counselor on this one!

I get lots and lots of fan mail. Arnold Lobel, who was a dear friend of mine, once told me, "Answer every one of those letters back." When I receive individual letters, I will answer the kid back. But when I get a class letter—and you can see the teacher wrote it on the blackboard—I usually answer the class.

LSM: Have you had running correspondences with certain children over the years?

JM: Quite a few. After about twelve, I lose them. They're very embarrassed to be even *seen* with me! Then when they're eighteen or nineteen, and they take kiddie-book courses in college, they start writing me again.

LSM: Really.

JM: Quite a few. I think it's fun. It's one of the nicer aspects. Sometimes it's a chore, if you don't work on the letters at least a little bit each day. There's always a big stack.

LSM: Do the children get very personal with you?

JM: Oh, yes, though I don't get any real horror stories. I think that because of the nature of my work, they're not going to tell me about awful things that happened to them.

LSM: Do kids ask you about how books are made? Do you find that they have many misconceptions?

JM: When I was a kid I didn't know that people made books. All kids now know that it comes from a person. I think when they're very little, they do not understand that there are multiple copies of a book, and that surprises them. But they're very sophisticated as a rule. I don't think they understand what happens at a printing press, but then neither do I. There's still some basic step that I can't quite get. When it goes into the stripping room, I sort of lose it.

LSM: Which of your characters do they like the best?

JM: George and Martha and the Stupids and Miss Nelson. Teachers all over the country are dressing up as Viola Swamp. I had one come to a book signing in California. She called me up at my apartment in San Francisco and said, "I've got this wonderful idea. I'm going to come dressed as Viola Swamp. While you're signing books, I'm going to beat you with a ruler!" I thought to myself, Oh, God, you know, I'm a grown man. Why did I get into this profession? And so I said, "This is not a good idea. First of all, there are going to be people there who aren't going to know who Viola Swamp is. This could only work—possibly—in a school setting." And she said: "Oh, I've got to do it, I've got to do it!" Finally, the day came. It was shaping up to be a very successful signing, with kids and adults all the way out the door. Then suddenly I heard this scream out on the street. I thought, well, she's *arrived*. She came tearing in. She was very successful, too. She looked just like the character. A little Japanese girl, maybe five, had just come up to me. I had signed her book, and somehow she was absolutely captured by the experience and was chewing on the tablecloth, looking up. And then she caught sight of this woman who had just come in and was hitting me over the head, you know, really pounding me with a ruler. And the little girl—well, they had to carry her out like a surfboard! She just froze. I think she's probably in therapy to this day. So I said to the teacher, "You see!" And the teacher said, "But isn't it *fun?*" It's great when a character catches on like that. We may do one more *Miss Nelson* book.

LSM: Many of your characters spend time looking for work—Fox in *Fox on the Job* (1988), Rapscallion Jones, and others.

JM: I've never thought about that. I guess I'm subconsciously afraid that my books will flop, and I'll have to be out looking for a job. I'm sure of that. I've always been afraid of that. I have the same dream that I'm sure everybody has, the dream of being back in school. And you've got that one test to take in chemistry and you forgot to study. And I find that if I don't have that dream, I have a variant of it, where I'm back teaching high school again, and I'm back with the nuns, and I have signed a fifty-year contract that I can't get out of, and I'll be in Cathedral High School for the rest of my life. And I wake up in a cold sweat, and I'm screaming, "But I want to publish books. I want to draw." And there's no one in the school, in the corridors. I'm probably living in the school. That will get me to the drawing table the next morning so fast! And I'll really do a good drawing. So it's probably a good thing, in a way.

LSM: One of the things I like about the folktale books you've been doing recently is the lightness you bring to them. It takes some of the weight off the stories that Bruno Bettelheim, for one, made everyone feel.

JM: The old fool! I think he's *wrong* half the time, and I also think he's, well . . . That's a tricky thing, to do those books. Obviously, I can't help trying to be funny. I don't know if I always am. I didn't want to distort the tales and lose the truth in them, but I thought they could be funny and light. At the same time I didn't want to go as far as the Disney version. And so I had to work very hard on them. I'm doing more, *Hansel and Gretel* (1990), which may be very tricky, from two points of view. You've got the horrid mother, and I've decided to push her hard, I mean in Roald Dahl's direction.

James Marshall •

Why soft-pedal it? She's a monster who wants to let her own children starve.

LSM: So, she won't be a stepmother?

JM: No. And I've got to push her to the hilt to make her grotesque. I'm not quite sure how I'm going to do that graphically.

LSM: You make the mother sound a little like Viola Swamp.

JM: Yes, but I don't want to do that, either. It's going to be hard work.

LSM: And what about the father? What will he be doing?

JM: He's going to be sort of not there. I had the same problem with the father in Cinderella. I had him always sleeping. I didn't want him to be an active character. And I didn't want him obviously to be watching all these horrible things happening and not doing anything about it. So I just had him sleep all the time. Maybe that's chickening out.

LSM: There's a lot more background detail in the fairy-tale books than, say, in the *George and Martha* ones.

JM: There's more background, but it's not realistic background. It's more like an elaborate stage set, I think. That forest in *Red Riding Hood* is supposed to look artificial. I don't know why I keep wanting things to look artificial. I guess because I can't draw naturalistically and also because the artificial has a more poetic resonance.

LSM: They look so different from your sparer drawings. I wonder if it has something to do with the fact that they're such old stories with so much tradition behind them.

JM: I'm sure.

LSM: And yet, some of the characters you've done in the past are very like characters found in the folktales—tricksters and fools.

JM: I like the tricksters. I like the fools. I like the old fool in Molière, who is one of my favorite writers. In *The Misanthrope,* for example. I love that kind of wily character. I think kids do, too.

LSM: Why do you think that is?

JM: Well, it's the fascination with masks. In the second *Miss Nelson* book, she changes God knows how many times. I think it's creating that face for the world. It's fun dressing up. Just for that alone. Turning the world into a play. They're very broad characters acting out very broad humor.

LSM: Many of your stories are about nervous anticipation: George and Martha worrying about what a scary movie will be like; Portly McSwine worrying about whether his party will be a success.

JM: I suppose that comes up from my own shabby character! As a sort of parody of my own character, and a lot of people I know— always projecting in the future. Gandhi said, "Never rehearse a tragedy." I must have rehearsed ten thousand. Only now, in my forties, have I learned to live in the present.

················

Robert McCloskey

Born September 15, 1914
Hamilton, Ohio

....

Robert McCloskey's *initial success as an illustrator came as the American picture book was riding the crest of its first golden age. His first book,* Lentil *(1940), appeared within a year of Ludwig Bemelmans'* Madeline *(1939) and H. A. Rey's* Curious George *(1941). With the publication of* Lentil, *McCloskey joined Viking editor May Massee's legendary corps of illustrators, a group that also included Bemelmans, Robert Lawson, Kurt Wiese, James Daugherty, and Ingri and Edgar Parin d'Aulaire.*

Massee's artists had an unrivaled knack for winning Caldecott Medals. McCloskey received his first Caldecott for his second picture book, Make Way for Ducklings, *in 1942, and won again for* Time of Wonder, *in 1958. The recipient as well of three Caldecott Honors, he retired in 1970 as one of the most celebrated artists in the history of the field. In 2000, the Library of Congress honored him with the designation of "Living Legend."* *

*Four other children's book authors and artists were so honored by the Library as part of its bicentennial celebration—Judy Blume, Beverly Cleary, Katherine Paterson, and Maurice Sendak.

Like film director Robert Capra and artist Norman Rockwell, McCloskey crafted gently satirical, upbeat narratives that expressed a deep-seated faith in the essential goodness of people. His books have endured in part because they reveal a timeless dimension in everyday scenes and experiences: the childhood rite of passage played out with a tooth and a feather in One Morning in Maine (1952); the universal urge to protect one's young in Make Way for Ducklings (1941). A reader closes a McCloskey book with a sense of gladness both for the comforting familiarity and awesome wonder of the world.

Portions of this interview were taped at the Weston Woods studios, Weston, Connecticut, on February 11, 1991, with additional material recorded by telephone on April 13 and November 4 of that year.

LEONARD S. MARCUS: Was reading important to you as a child?

ROBERT McCLOSKEY: It's hard to remember a time when there weren't very many children's books. But in our public library in Hamilton, Ohio, for instance, when I was a boy, one shelf would accommodate all of the children's books that they had, and a lot of those were duplicates. The good ones I remember were the Dr. Doolittles and one Winnie-the-Pooh. Later, when I was writing Homer Price (1943), I was really writing down the stories that I thought kids would like that I didn't find there on the shelf when I was a child.

LSM: I've heard you were something of a boy inventor.

RMcC: My grandfather was a tinkerer, and as a child I made our Christmas tree revolve and tried to build a cotton-candy machine out of a vacuum-cleaner motor and a dishpan. I poured sugar into my device thinking it would spin the sugar out as I'd seen it done at carnivals, but it didn't. Then I figured I had to melt the sugar, and as I didn't have the know-how for that, I poured molasses into my machine as the equivalent of sugar already melted. But the molasses just spun out all over the kitchen and all over me. I must have been upward of ten when I did that.

Going back earlier, I remember when electricity arrived in our house. I was about three then. I don't recall anything about switches, but I do remember the difference in the quality of the light.

I was very interested in any news item about Edison, and I went through a long period of building model airplanes. I taught other boys soap carving and model-plane building at the YMCA.

Later, in the army during the war, I invented a machine for folding sticky tape and a machine for flipping over field charts. But the army had no place for an artist, so they used to hide me. They'd put me on a truck and send me off into the hills.

LSM: Did art interest you as a child?

RMcC: Yes, but I couldn't make up my mind what I might end up being. I played the piano and oboe and, at one time, thought of becoming a musician. I had a harmonica band, which performed at local lodge meetings and church socials. *Lentil*, my first published book, is a spin-off of that.

LSM: Did your parents encourage your artistic side?

RMcC: They did, but I think they would have been much happier if I had chosen a career in, say, engineering.

Hamilton was the center of the universe to me. I had been nowhere else, except to a summer resort on Lake Erie for family vacations, and I'd spent part of a summer on a farm in Indiana. *National Geographic* and *The Saturday Evening Post* and the Sears and Roebuck catalog were big sources of information about the outside world. Somehow—I don't know how—I got the idea that if I were a successful artist I could live anywhere I wanted to. Then, in high school, I got a scholarship to go to art school in Boston. The depression had begun, and but for that scholarship I think I would never have been able to set foot out of the state of Ohio.

LSM: Was *Lentil*, with its affectionate portrait of small-town America, your farewell to Hamilton?

RMcC: No, I didn't think of it as that. I didn't think of *Lentil* as being about an exact place. I used bits and pieces of my hometown. The monuments and other buildings are composites, slightly caricatured. The 1930s was the time of American Scene art, when artists were becoming eager to depict typically American subjects instead of just European or classical ones. *Lentil* was connected to that. As a boy I had suspenders and dressed rather like my story's hero, though my mother would never permit barefootedness.

LSM: Were there flimflam men in Hamilton, like the ones you wrote about in *Homer Price*?

RMcC: There used to be a Saturday market around the courthouse in the town square, where farmers would sell their produce. Along with the farmers, these other people would show up selling things like snake oil—it must have been lubricating oil or something that they doctored up. And corn removers—all sold by con men. I used to listen to those people by the hour with their medicine shows.

LSM: What got you started making children's books?

RMcC: Well, one of my boyhood friends was a nephew of the editor May Massee. When I was growing up with him I heard about his aunt, so that was one of my introductions to the field. Once I became interested in children's books, Miss Massee was the first person I went to see.

When I came east from Hamilton, I had only the germ of an idea for *Lentil*. It started out as just a lot of pictures of a boy playing the harmonica. I didn't have any idea whether I was going to have words with my pictures or not. I thought the drawings might lead to a series of lithographic prints, not necessarily to a children's book at all. But once there got to be some words, the words grew and then the pictures grew. For a time, it just seemed to go on forever, with no beginning or end. But when I met May Massee it fell into place.

LSM: Did the art school you attended in Boston offer a course in children's book illustration?

RMcC: They had a course in illustration but not children's book illustration. I don't think that anyone had a special course for that then. In those days, you illustrated whatever came along. *The Saturday Evening Post* was the top. If you could get an illustration job from the *Post*, you had arrived! Artists were also very happy to get a job from *Fortune* magazine. In those days, if you were in Provincetown over the summer and somebody sold a drawing or print, everybody in town knew about it, and all your friends would gather round and you'd have to treat them. If you sold a painting, it was almost, "May I touch you?!"

LSM: You set your next book, *Make Way for Ducklings*, in Boston, where you yourself had gone to live.

RMcC: *Ducklings* was a spin-off, too. I had gotten a job as an artist's assistant painting murals of Boston subjects—the State House, the Charles River, Louisburg Square. So these were all subjects I had been thinking about in terms of spatial relationships and scale, and it seemed just natural right after that to put those subjects down on the page.

LSM: Wasn't *Make Way for Ducklings* also based on a true story that had been reported in the Boston papers?

RMcC: Yes, and one time I saw those ducklings myself, on the curb having come across the street to the Boston Public Garden, though not with the police and everyone looking on, as in my story.

LSM: I've always thought the story started off in a curious way, with a family of wild animals moving to a big city in search of a safe place to live.

RMcC: In those days, ducks might have had a better chance in Boston. At one time, my late wife and I had a house on a pond in

Bedford, New York, where we saw swans disappear, taken by the turtles.

LSM: How did work on *Make Way for Ducklings* proceed?

RMcC: By then I'd moved from Boston to a studio apartment in New York City, and though I returned to Boston to make sketches, it was cold weather and rainy and very unpleasant. I soon realized I couldn't study ducks there. Then an ornithologist mentioned that I could buy live ducks at a certain Greenwich Village market. So I did—I brought them home and kept them in the tub, though not continuously. Once in a while I had to make use of that tub myself! The ducklings were not hard to manage when they were young, but their appetites and size increased very rapidly.

LSM: You made an unusual choice in having the whole book, text and illustrations, printed in brown ink.

RMcC: It had to be as interesting as I could make it because I didn't have enough of a reputation then for them to take a chance on printing a big book like that in full color. I made the original lithographic drawings in black and white. The ink used in the printing gave them a sepia color. Black and white just seemed such a cold thing for a children's book—and for those ducks. Later when I got to *Blueberries for Sal* (1948), I wondered if I could get away with that blue ink, and I didn't make up my mind till the last minute.

It was a time of experiment, and artists had to be a lot more involved in the graphic process in those days. The publisher would never have been able to afford to put out a book like *Make Way for Ducklings* for two bucks if I hadn't been very involved. They saved on the platemaking.

I stretched all my know-how to the limit in just making the lithographic plates. I debated, for a while, whether to do the illustrations in woodcuts or wood engravings rather than lithographs, but when I found out that they would probably take what I had done and print them by lithographic process, it seemed a silly thing for me not to do the lithographs myself. So *Ducklings*, like *Lentil* before it, was done as lithographic drawings on the zinc, though they made transfers from those to put on the printing plates. I never used stones for lithography, as the d'Aulaires did, because that's such a storage job.

LSM: *Make Way for Ducklings* is such a good title. Did you think of it right away?

RMcC: No, I didn't think of it at all, as a matter of fact. I think I called it something like *Boston Is Lovely in the Spring*. It was Miss Massee's secretary who thought up a title for it.

LSM: Your career was really taking off just then. You had recently won two major art awards unrelated to your work as a children's book illustrator, the Prix de Rome* for your watercolors and a Tiffany Foundation Prize.

RMcC: Yes, and one day the publicity person from Viking called up and said, "*Life* magazine wants to come down to your studio." *Life* was everything in those days. The photographer arrived and took pictures of the ducks, me drawing them, and me playing harmonica with the ducks quacking all over me. Those were wild times. The *Life* article was due to be published when the entire issue was suddenly scrapped—boom! like that—because Hitler had just invaded Poland.

LSM: The sense of warmth, which you spoke about a moment ago, carries over to your detailed depiction of Boston.

RMcC: I was meticulous about pursuing accuracy, though it's not a matter of measurements: it was the feel of Boston, a place I enjoyed, that I wanted. No one is going to go strolling or flying over and

*McCloskey won this award in 1939, but did not take his year of study at the American Academy in Rome until 1948.

check the number of chimneys that I put on or the number of bricks. But the detail of a wrought-iron fence, for instance, that a child would put his hand on or walk right by or rub a stick on in the way children do—that's accurate.

LSM: The drawings also have amazing energy.

RMcC: Children like to pore over pictures. And in those days, as I said, I thought of myself as a mural painter. I wanted to cover walls. I found it confining to scale down my pictures and ideas to put them inside the pages of a book. So I tried every trick I could to get as much into those pictures as possible. I paced the illustrations and gave them a variety of viewpoints—aerial views and others— to create a sense of space and movement and a feeling of something going on.

LSM: Like the boy racing by on his bicycle like a bat out of hell . . .

RMcC: Yes.

LSM: Were you surprised by the success of *Make Way for Ducklings?*

RMcC: Yes, I was. I was surprised by the Caldecott Medal because I had never heard of it. Of course, that award had only been around for a few years then.

LSM: Do you still like the book now?

RMcC: Sometimes I wake up at night from a dream of being in a warehouse full of books! Forklifts and trucks full of thousands of copies of the book, and all of them are printed with exactly the same mistakes. You have an eye that's slightly out of place and that offends you when you see it. It gets to be like a drippy faucet. Now I have to force that out.

With *Ducklings*, I feel a great responsibility of having unleashed something. I get letters from children from all over the world and a lot of pictures of ducks. People also send me postcards and photographs they've taken of ducklings crossing a road with their mother and cars stopping for them. This is something that happens all over

Robert McCloskey

the world. It doesn't know any national or continental boundaries.

LSM: Do you think that's why *Make Way for Ducklings* has lasted?

RMcC: People see a lot of different things in that book. It never occurred to me that it would be taken as exemplary of family life. But there must be some sort of reassurance in a story about a father mallard making a promise to return, and then keeping that promise. I couldn't begin to explain it.

Then there are other people who have used *Ducklings* to train children to stop and look in both directions before they cross the street—just traffic know-how. It has, of course, also been an introductory book to Boston for many people.

All my books have somehow gone off and found their own level. There have been libraries that installed reading corners—or "reading nooks," which got to be a big thing at one time—and they would require an old boat, for instance, like Burt Dow's, and upholster it and paint it. Or they would have a bathtub with claw feet like Lentil's. To make it comfortable it must have had a soft cozy lining—perhaps even a mattress and some pillows.

I never expected those books to be so popular. Nor did the publisher! And no one could tell that children's books were going to be as widely accepted as they have become.

LSM: *Blueberries for Sal*, your first book set in Maine, has an almost musical form. It's a two-part invention in which the bears' and humans' berry-picking adventures become entwined.

RMcC: I'd never thought of it like that, but it is a sort of counterpoint, isn't it? One day I had taken my wife and daughter blueberrying and had taken along my sketchbook and was just lazing there, almost dozing away in the sun, when I heard this *kerplink, kerplank, kerplunk* of the berries striking the bottom of Sal's pail. I guess that that was what set the whole thing off—not music, but a *kerplink!* inviting you to sing along.

LSM: Did bears come along, as happens in the story?

RMcC: No, the bears were imagined, though meeting up with bears in Maine while blueberrying used to be a pretty common occurrence.

It's odd. A lot of my books are of a locale. The locale of *Lentil* is Ohio—but I did that book in New York City. I think I made the first draft of *Ducklings*, which is about Boston, in Connecticut, and I finished it in New York City. And here was *Blueberries for Sal*, this story of Maine, and when I finally got around to starting the drawings for it, we were staying in suburban New York. I researched blueberry plants at the New York Botanical Garden and went to the Central Park Zoo to sketch the bears.

LSM: You have said that when you first saw Maine you liked what you saw. What in particular about Maine appealed to you?

RMcC: Maine is just a beautiful spot. It gives you an opportunity to get the cobwebs of a place like New York out of your hair and time to observe.

LSM: Your books are filled with similar reminders of the rewards of close observation—Sal's discovery of a "magic" feather in *One Morning in Maine* (1952), the children's sighting of a hummingbird in *Time of Wonder*.

RMcC: I think there is a lot of satisfaction in allowing your eye to go roving over the surface of a thing, or an illustration in a book, knowing and imagining and realizing what connects what, and why.

LSM: In your second Caldecott Medal acceptance speech, given in 1958—the year after *Sputnik* and a time of a great clamoring for better science education—you spoke out on behalf of the need for better art education. Why?

RMcC: People—adults as well as children—so often just don't realize what they're looking at. There's no thought behind it. They'll say to themselves, "Well, that's a bookshelf," or "That's an ele-

Robert McCloskey

phant," and see nothing other than just the fact. There's no sense of relationship—of the relationship of a house to its environment, a man to his environment, of the scale of things. Our understanding of cause and effect is disappearing because people are doing so much looking without evaluating. Television adds to this with all the tricks they can do. Seeing is really a decision-making process, a matter of evaluating what is around you. And children cannot develop that ability so well as they can by learning to draw.

LSM: The *Ducklings* sculpture in the Boston Public Garden is just the right size for small children to climb on.

RMcC: It was very difficult to decide how large they should be. They're tremendous compared to actual ducklings. I saw the bronze figures for the first time in the sculptor's studio, and when they're indoors they look tremendous. It was a shock to me. So I said, "Well, we'll have to take them out." So we put them on a dolly and got them out in the snow and off under some trees, and took a look—and they were just great. Now I have lots of photographs of people and their children with the sculpture in the garden. I never thought it would happen, but in a very short time, those ducklings have found a life of their own.

....

Iona Opie

Born October 13, 1923
Colchester, England

....

I ona and Peter Opie happened onto their
life's work when, as a young couple expecting their first child, they chanced to recall the
nursery rhyme that begins, "Ladybird, ladybird,
/ Fly away home," and wondered about its
history. Not everyone, of course, would have
followed up on a moment's curiosity first by
heading to the library to track down everything
known about that particular rhyme's origins,
and then by doing the same for hundreds more

from the Mother Goose canon. But the Opies were a thorough as well as
a fortunate pair. When their Oxford Dictionary of Nursery Rhymes
(1951) was published seven years later, the baby boom was on, and the
couple's efforts were enthusiastically greeted by war-weary readers
intrigued to learn that nursery nonsense was in fact a treasure trove of
English wisdom, wit, and lore.

In their second and several subsequent books, the freelancing Opies
turned their attention to playground rhymes and the games associated
with them. As a research aid, they amassed a world-class collection of
early children's books (now at the Bodleian Library, Oxford), and a companion hoard—from bibs to bicycles—of childhood artifacts. In all their

work, the Opies continued to make the point that one of the best ways to know a culture is by paying attention to its children's games and pastimes.

An exacting scholar with a warm, informal manner, Iona Opie is equally at home at the British Library and her local schoolyard, an hour's drive south of London. In recent years, she has completed much of the work left unfinished at the time of Peter Opie's death in 1982 and has edited a new generation of Mother Goose books aimed at children's delight.

We recorded our conversation at New York's Algonquin Hotel on October 21, 1988, during Iona Opie's first visit to the United States following her husband's death six years earlier.

LEONARD S. MARCUS: How did *The Oxford Dictionary of Nursery Rhymes* come about?

IONA OPIE: Ah, the story about the famous ladybird, who helped us at the time that we were expecting our first child. It was due to this ladybird that we started our whole life's work. She is more or less the heraldic beast of the Opie family. But before I tell that story, perhaps I should go back a bit further, because the actual beginning of our work, of course, was our getting married.

Peter had written three autobiographies by the time I married him—two and a half, actually; he finished the third after we were married. He was twenty-four then. And as the books brought in almost no money at all, the elders of the family told him he must get a proper job. So he joined a publisher of reference works just off Fleet Street in London. But toward the end of the war, work became difficult in London because of all the bombs.

LSM: It must have been incredibly frightening.

IO: It was. They were terrible. There were the buzz bombs and the rockets. The buzz bombs were the worst because they were pilotless planes with this curiously relentless chugging noise. You knew that at any moment the engine was going to cut out and they would fall and the bomb would go off, leaving a huge crater behind.

LSM: A sort of roll of the dice.

IO: Yes, exactly. The whole of Peter's firm was evacuated down to the country, and I had already been dismissed by the WAAFs (Women's Auxiliary Air Force) because we were expecting our first child. So I was also down in the country. We were rather at a loose end and used to go for long country walks. On one of these walks, we were walking down the side of a cornfield and found a ladybird and automatically put it on our—I forget whose finger it was; somebody's finger—and said its rhyme to it, and suddenly saw the rhyme quite dispassionately. It was hardly a narrative, but at any rate it seemed a very curious thing to say to the ladybird:

> Ladybird, ladybird,
>> Fly away home.
> Your house is on fire
>> And your children all gone;
> All except for one
>> And that's little Ann,
> And she has crept under
>> The warming pan.

Peter and I always took up anything that happened to us and wanted to know everything about it, and, as I say, we were expecting our first child and therefore had become intensely interested in the things of childhood. So we wondered where the "Ladybird" rhyme came from, and the next time we went up to London, we went to the local public library. We were sure that there would be a reference book which would tell us the history of the rhyme. There

Iona Opie

was a reference book, but it was published in 1842 and it didn't tell us all we wanted to know. So we felt there might be room for another book and simply followed up the clues in the earlier one, J. O. Halliwell's *Nursery Rhymes of England*, and took it as far as we possibly could. We had no idea then that it was going to take us seven years to finish what turned out to be *The Oxford Dictionary of Nursery Rhymes*.

LSM: I have read a letter that Peter Opie wrote you before you were married, in which he said: "Can this indescribable war fit in with the theory of human progress?" Did the irrationality and horror of the war draw you to nonsense as a possible source of alternative truths?

IO: Peter wrote that letter in reply to my writing him about his idealistic autobiography—the first one. He had had to change his rather naive hopes for humanity. We were all so broken up by the wickedness of that war. It was a particularly evil war. All through my life, more and more, I've realized that nursery rhymes and nonsense like Lewis Carroll's *Alice* books give one buoyancy that makes life bearable. For instance, I brought *Alice's Adventures Through the Looking Glass* with me on this trip as a sort of antidote to being in a strange country, because I know that life is irrational, surrealistic, and that it's all happened before, this upside downness and living backward and all these ways one thinks one has to adapt to.

LSM: You have written about Mother Goose rhymes as a still-evolving tradition.

IO: There are always extra rhymes coming along and being adopted by Mother Goose, if they're worthy. The qualification is that a rhyme has to be anonymous and memorable and have some use, even if it's only a nonsense use. Some nonsense rhymes simply make you feel happier than you were before. This one, for instance, does wonders for me: "Gaily the troubadour / Walks round the waterbutt

The following gallery of illustrations and page layouts
samples the work of each artist and writer interviewed in these
pages. In making this small selection from the thousands
of possibilities, I have kept three goals in mind:
to suggest something of the development, range, and flavor
of each person's work; to highlight certain key books
and key points about those books, as raised in our conversations;
and, perhaps most important, to entice readers to go back
to the books to which the images belong—the better
to experience them as they were meant to be seen and read.

L. S. M.

FROM: *Anno's Alphabet: An Adventure in Imagination*
by Mitsumasa Anno
1974

FROM: *Anno's Journey*
by Mitsumasa Anno
1977

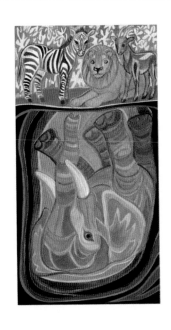

The People lived in the hills, not daring to go into the forest for fear that Elephant would crush them with his great strength.

Then it happened one day that Elephant fell into a great pit. Try as he might, he could not pull himself up. Nor was any other creature strong enough to pull him up. Many thought it was the end of Elephant.

FROM: *The Story of the Three Kingdoms*
by **Walter Dean Myers**
illustrated by **Ashley Bryan**
1995

When Granny Anika finally came out of her dance right side up, she was eleven miles north of her village.

FROM: *The Dancing Granny*
retold and illustrated by
Ashley Bryan
1977

In the light of the moon
a little egg lay on a leaf.

FROM: *The Very Hungry Caterpillar*
by Eric Carle
1969
·····························

d evening! whirred a dragonfly,
ing above the water.
little cricket wanted to answer.
e rubbed his wings together.
nothing happened. Not a sound.

FROM: *The Very Quiet Cricket*
by Eric Carle
1990

"Brown Bear,
Brown Bear,
What do you see?"

"I see a redbird
looking at me."

FROM: *Brown Bear, Brown Bear, What Do You See?*
by Bill Martin, Jr., 1967
re-illustrated by Eric Carle
1983

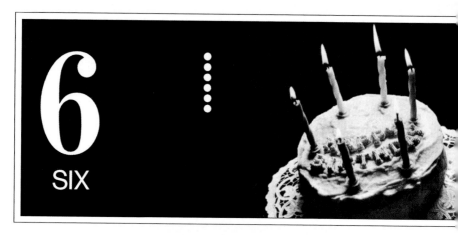

6
SIX

FROM: *Count and See*
by Tana Hoban
1972

FROM: *Exactly the Opposite*
by Tana Hoban
1990

All the men put on black socks. There are short socks and long socks and fancy silk socks that have decorations called clocks. Some of the men wear leg garters to keep the long socks from falling down around their ankles.

FROM: *The Philharmonic Gets Dressed*
by **Karla Kuskin**
Illustrated by Marc Simont
1982
....

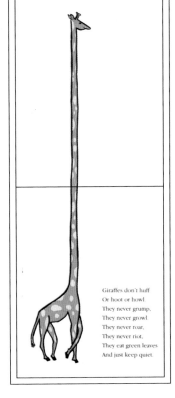

Giraffes don't huff
Or hoot or howl.
They never grump.
They never growl.
They never roar.
They never riot.
They eat green leaves
And just keep quiet.

FROM: *Roar and More*
by **Karla Kuskin**
1956
....

FROM: *Goldilocks and the Three Bears*
retold and illustrated by James Marshall
1988

....

FROM: *Miss Nelson Has a Field Day*
by Harry Allard
illustrated by James Marshall
1985

....

right on into the Public Garden.

FROM: *Make Way for Ducklings*
by **Robert McCloskey**
1941

"Maybe we can find my tooth where it dropped," said Sal, hopefully feeling around in the muddy gravel where the clams live.

Sal's father helped her look, but a muddy tooth looks so much like a muddy pebble, and a muddy pebble looks so much like a muddy tooth, that they hunted and hunted without finding it.

"We'll have to stop looking and take our clams back to the house, Sal," her father said at last, "or we won't have time for the trip to the village." He washed off the clams in the clean salt water of the bay, and Sal reluctantly stopped looking and waded in to wash the mud from her feet and hands.

"I guess some clam will find my tooth and get what I wished for," said Sal. "If we come back here tomorrow and find a clam eating a chocolate ice-cream cone, why, we'll have to take it away from him and make him give my tooth back too," she said.

FROM: *One Morning in Maine*
by **Robert McCloskey**
1952

FROM: *Eating Out*
by Helen
Oxenbury
1983

Splash splosh!
Splash splosh!
Splash splosh!

FROM: *We're Going on a Bear Hunt*
retold by Michael Rosen
illustrated by Helen Oxenbury
1989

John Henry offered to lend them a hand.

"That's all right. We'll put some dynamite to it."

John Henry smiled to himself. "Whatever you say."

The road crew planted dynamite all around the rock and set it off.

KERBOOM BLAMMITY-BLAMMITY BOOMBOOM BANGBOOMBANG!!!

That dynamite made so much racket, the Almighty looked over the parapets of Heaven and hollered, "It's getting too noisy down there." The dynamite kicked up so much dirt and dust, it got dark. The moon thought night had caught her napping and she hurried out so fast, she almost bumped into the sun who was still climbing the steep hill toward noontime.

When all the commotion from the dynamite was over, the road crew was amazed. The boulder was still there. In fact, the dynamite hadn't knocked even a chip off it.

FROM: *John Henry*
by Julius Lester
illustrated by Jerry Pinkney
1994

FROM:
The Talking Eggs
by Robert D. San Souci
illustrated by
Jerry Pinkney
1989

FROM: *A Hole Is To Dig: A First Book of First Definitions*
by Ruth Krauss
illustrated by
Maurice Sendak
1952

....

FROM: *In the Night Kitchen*
by Maurice Sendak
1970

....

—24—

FROM: *I Saw Esau: The Schoolchild's Pocket Book*
edited by Iona and Peter Opie
illustrated by Maurice Sendak
1992

....

It really was cold outside, very cold. The wind whirled the falling snow-flakes about, this way, that way, and into Irene's squinting face. She set out on the uphill path to Farmer Bennett's sheep pasture.

By the time she got there, the snow was up to her ankles and the wind was worse. It hurried her along and made her stumble. Irene resented this; the box was problem enough. "Easy does it!" she cautioned the wind, leaning back hard against it.

FROM: *Brave Irene*
by William Steig
1986

They could guess what he was dreaming about. Mrs. De Soto handed her husband a pole to keep the fox's mouth open.

FROM: *Doctor De Soto*
by William Steig
1982

Father played with Kate,

Father played with Kate.

FROM: *Noisy Nora*
by **Rosemary Wells**
1973, 1997

....

FROM:
My Very First Mother Goose
edited by **Iona Opie**
illustrated by **Rosemary Wells**
1996

....

FROM: *The Storm Book*
by **Charlotte Zolotow**
illustrated by Margaret Bloy Graham
1952

....

FROM: *William's Doll*
by **Charlotte Zolotow**
illustrated by
William Pène du Bois
1972

....

William wanted a doll.
He wanted to hug it
and cradle it in his arms

5

/ Softly a brickbat / Hits him on the coconut." Another rhyme was told me by one of the illustrators of *Tail Feathers from Mother Goose* (1988), Caroline Anstey:

> There was a man who always wore
> a saucepan on his head.
> I asked him what he did it for.
> "I don't know why," he said.
>
> "It always makes my ears so sore.
> I am a foolish man.
> I think I'll have to take it off
> And wear a frying pan."

She suddenly said she'd known it all her life and loved it. It's a kind of punch line, you see. You're expecting him to wear a Trilby instead.

LSM: Have you heard any new rhymes since your arrival in New York a few days ago?

IO: I collected one from the head of Little, Brown. These rhymes, you see, always ameliorate a situation. They're like a balm being poured on a sore place. In the new rhyme, a crisis is identified: Someone has found a fly in his soup. So the antidote, as so often occurs, is a nonsense rhyme. The person who is putting the situation right says: "Please don't shout / Or wave it about / Or the rest / Will be wanting one, too." Isn't that nice? The whole thing is going to dissolve into laughter. That's what nonsense does, I think. It dissolves. It relaxes. Especially if you can laugh at yourself you feel much better immediately.

Every time I broadcast, people write in to say that they have got their own family rhyme—"heirloom rhymes," we call them—that they have inherited through several generations, and that they don't want to die out. We have become a sort of archive for Mother Goose rhymes, where they will be kept safely. Eventually they're all going to the Bodleian Library at Oxford.

LSM: Were you already familiar with some version of the rhyme about the saucepan that you recited a moment ago?

IO: No, I'd never met it before. I believe that a lot of the best nonsense rhymes ultimately derive from the music hall and from pantomime songs. The poor people of London used to go to the music halls and would be regaled with sturdy nonsense making fun of things like husbands getting drunk and the baby crying all night. They would come back feeling better, and they would go on singing parts of the songs, especially the choruses. Then when they were grandparents, they would amuse their grandchildren with the songs as they remembered them, and they became family possessions. There must be hundreds more in families that I know nothing about.

LSM: Was there an idea of "high culture" and "low culture" which may have rendered your discovery about the origins of the rhymes disillusioning to some people, who had imagined a loftier history for them?

IO: I don't know. Nursery rhymes run right through the social strata. Everybody knows the same main canon of nursery rhymes. If one of the MPs in the Houses of Parliament refers to "Humpty Dumpty," everybody knows what he means. The *Alice* books are used that way, too, with very brief allusions about how to make a word mean just what you like, and so on. It is a lingua franca, really.

LSM: There have been many attempts at reading various allegorical meanings into some of the rhymes.

IO: Yes, well that was a game in itself. We stopped being cross about it after a while, because people so loved these little stories, which are folklore stories about folklore, really. There's a perpetual argument whether "Ring-a-ring o' roses" was really about the Great Plague of London, and people learned all the different meanings, the different bits, you know. The ring of roses was a rosy rash which was one of the symptoms of the Plague—which it was not, of course! There were black spots. There were no rosy rashes. But people learn these details, and they feel it's romantic for some reason, even though it's such a grisly subject. They also feel rather clever at remembering the meanings in the four different parts of the rhyme. I remember sitting next to a girl in the ballet who said, "Oh yes. I know 'Ring-a-ring o' roses' is all about the Plague." And I said in response, "There is not a shred of evidence." And I can still remember the disappointment in her voice as she said, "Oh." Terrible!

LSM: Peter Opie said in an interview once that he didn't like names—the names of things. If names lock our awareness of reality into too fixed a form, might not another of the "uses" of nonsense be to tamper a bit with the locks, to expand perception?

IO: If you get rid of the usual name, it helps you to look with quite a new eye. This happens to the oldest riddles, such as "Humpty Dumpty" and the Orkney prose riddles, when a fire can be seen as the "little cow in the corner, who eats all." Nonsense names are a great defense of the underdog, too. To call the highest person in the land "Great Panjandrum" immediately alters that person's status; it makes the underdog more nearly equal to the overdog. It punctures pomposity and is a very big boost to the ego, if you're afraid of something.

There are rhymes for when children are misbehaving, say at the dinner table, that create fun instead of making the children feel guilty: "You musn't look / You musn't stare / You musn't wave / Your fork in the air." We used to say it to our children. It doesn't have to be very clever, which that isn't. But if you can say it in rhyme, the

Iona Opie

rhyme itself makes the instruction seem old, as if it has been going on forever. It makes it impersonal. "This is a traditional rhyme. It's not especially for this occasion." It's just got authority from years gone by, so the child doesn't mind but stops waving his fork in the air.

LSM: It's also entertaining. Is it possible to identify the earliest appearances of humor in children's literature?

IO: Well, yes. It arrived via the nursery rhymes—the scraps of non-sense songs which had been used to entertain children and were then printed in little booklets for children—*Tommy Thumb's Song Book* (1744), and the like. The chapbook printers sometimes filled their sixteen-page booklets by adding fifteen more verses to a well-known nursery rhyme—"Little Tommy Tucker," for instance—to make a longer narrative. Sarah Catherine Martin did the same thing when she wrote and illustrated *The Comic Adventures of Old Mother Hubbard*—only the first three verses were traditional. Her little book was an immense success when John Harris published it in 1805, and he went on to produce a long series of book-lets, all lighthearted. It was through a booklet of this type that Edward Lear became acquainted with the limerick. A friend read him "There was a sick man of Tobago" out of *The Anecdotes and Adventures of Fifteen Gentlemen* (1821), published by Harris's rival John Marshall. After Lear, of course, nonsense was well away.

LSM: In children's literature, historically, there has always been a tug-of-war between the impulse to entertain and the impulse to instruct. You refer to this in your introduction to *A Nursery Companion* (1980), noting that the Regency period in England was a time of joyousness and frivolity in children's books, and that in suc-ceeding years the pendulum swung the other way. Of the latter period, you say: "The belief in progress, and the possible perfectibility of man, was once again to take hold of men's minds; and, as always

WAYS OF TELLING

in periods of moral advancement, lightheartedness was to be frowned upon."

IO: Yes, after the Regency, reality and moral pressures returned. Children were reproved for vanity, urged to be obedient, clean, and industrious, and above all, shown—in numerous tales—the consequences of telling lies. Throughout all of early children's literature, lying seems to have been considered the most heinous sin.

LSM: So then Heinrich Hoffmann in Germany and Edward Lear in England represented the next wave of rebelliousness against didacticism.

IO: Yes. Hoffmann wrote *Struwwelpeter* (1845) to amuse his young patients because he thought the didactic books they had to read were not improving their health. A lot of people are very frightened by Hoffmann, aren't they? All those bleeding thumbs, when Kaspar has his thumb cut off by the scissor-man because he was sucking it. People still have nightmares about that. But nonsense, if you take it as nonsense, is very bracing. You can turn practically anything into a comic situation, and if you have enough comedy in your own life that has not been associated with pain and real distress, then it is possible to turn real distress, when it happens, back into comedy. Rather like the Duke of Wellington when he lost his leg at Waterloo. Somebody remarked, "Oh, you lost your leg." And he said, "By Jove, sir, I have!"

LSM: A child's reaction to Hoffmann's book may depend on the reaction of the parent who is reading it with the child.

IO: It's very important for parents to read to their children with their children in their lap and their arms round them, and then they are both reading the story. If the parent is taking it as a bit of a joke, so will the child.

LSM: One of the main qualities of the Mother Goose rhymes, as well as of the nonsense books of Hoffmann, Lear, and Carroll, is that they are fiercely unsentimental.

IO: Yes, indeed. None of the nonsense rhymes are sentimental. They are very realistic. And then there are the teasing rhymes. When a child is teased with any of those rhymes, he thinks that he is being attacked personally, because he doesn't know that the rhyme is old. You know: "Smarty, smarty / Gave a party. / Nobody came." The child thinks that that applies to him only. Later on when they read our books, you see, they find out they weren't the only ones! It comforts teachers, too, as well as children, to find that those nasty rhymes about teachers have been going on for generations.

I think it is awful when you first go to school and realize that life is not all kindness such as you have had at home, if you were lucky; that people actually want to irritate you. So you do this comic thing of losing your temper. Temper is always comic, isn't it? So you have betrayed yourself twice: You have allowed yourself to be needled, and you have made yourself ridiculous.

LSM: Were nonsense rhymes an important part of your own childhood?

IO: My mother was very sweet and absolutely serious and didn't like people to lose their tempers and didn't like nonsense herself. So I really missed out. I was a deprived child. I found the outside world very, very hard and painful at first. I didn't know any of the funny answers, you see, to say back. You have got to know the answers: "Sticks and stones may break my bones but names will never hurt me." If I had known that when I was young, I could have turned it off. Somebody comes up and says, "Gonna fight you," and the answer to that is to say scornfully, "You and who else?" Traditional backchat is marvelous. There is always a weapon against whatever weapon is thrust at you, and you have got to know what it is because there is very little time to think of anything original. You usually think of it a half hour later when the whole occasion is over. So the ready-made repartee is very very useful to a child.

LSM: *The Lord of the Flies* was published in 1954, three years after *The Oxford Dictionary of Nursery Rhymes*, and during the period that you were at work on your next book, *The Lore and Language of Schoolchildren* (1959). Did Golding's novel influence your way of looking at children, especially as his characters spanned the same age range as those whose games you were then studying?

IO: Peter reacted against *The Lord of the Flies*. He believed in children's ability to get on with each other, but I thought that if they were confined on that island, they would have turned savage. When children have too small a space, they do turn on one another like animals in too small a cage. But he said, no, they would have created their own government quite amicably. We always disagreed on that one. You see, one of the troubles of talking about children is that each child is a different individual, so if you have an evil, monstrous person like Jack, who became power mad, he would probably terrorize the others. But equally on that plane that crashed there might not have been one of those Stalin types. It is difficult to resist evil because evil is so egotistical. It is not going to take into account anybody else's feelings.

LSM: When *The Lore and Language of Schoolchildren* appeared in 1959, Penelope Mortimer's review of the book in the *London Evening Standard* was headlined: "CHILDREN—THEY'RE ALL LITTLE SAVAGES!" Among other things she said, "I can't help being disturbed (to put it mildly) that in all these four hundred close-packed pages there is hardly a game, prank or custom that is not based on savagery or violence." Do you think that *The Lord of the Flies* affected, to any great extent, the public's reception of *The Lore and Language of Schoolchildren* or of your subsequent books?

IO: It is curious that *The Lord of the Flies*, which had been published five years before and was a sensation, did not seem to have prepared people at all for the gruesome and violent nature of children's group life. If that book did not prepare them, then surely they should have been prepared by memories of their own childhood—though childhood memories, especially if they are painful, tend to be set aside. When the paperback of *The Lore and Language* came out, it was featured on a television book program. Sir Hugh Casson, who was on the panel, refused to discuss it. When asked for his opinion, an expression of extreme distaste passed over his face, and all he said was, "It brings back my own schooldays far too clearly—I shall not say anything more." But you have to bear two things in mind. One is that a child who is quite civilized on his own, or in his own family, can turn into a bully and a demon when having to maintain his ego in a crowd. And the other is that some of the school lore—the scatological rhymes and the tales of horror and death—are only therapeutic (and they are therapeutic) when recited, and giggled over, by a whole bunch of kids of about the same age. That creates a kind of communal courage.

LSM: I wonder if you would talk about the general characteristics of children's games?

IO: They've got an outlined set of rules which must be adhered to. Children are very strict about that. There are variations which are allowed by common consent if the idea is thought good. The game rhymes have an element of fantasy in them. They are also playlets, some of them, like the one that goes: "Please Mr. Crocodile, / May we cross the water / To see your ugly daughter?" The children are playing a role in that game, and that is fun because they know it is ridiculous. It takes the lid off the whole school day.

LSM: Why did you decide to study state-educated children only?

IO: We used the state schools for our surveys because the children tend to follow local traditions in games and lore, and we wanted to plot local customs and words on distribution maps—words like the truce terms, which they use when they want to stop playing for a moment in a chasing game. Local private schools take children from—as they say now—upwardly mobile families, who move around more. Of course, this was truer in the 1950s than it is today. In the south of England especially, local distinctions have become blurred in all the schools.

LSM: Why do you think it is that child lore "flourishes best," as you've written, in cities?

IO: Ah! Well, people seem to be surprised that this is so. There are many more children in cities, and they are packed closer together. The city acts as a sort of pressure pot for games. It has a shifting population, and there's a rapid exchange of games and rhymes and jokes between children playing in—say—the playgrounds attached to London churches, or in the spaces between blocks of flats. And because the children are crammed together, they have to assert themselves—have to compete to take charge of a game, and be quicker with the repartee. Little termagants, some of them. In the country, people are more spread out, and in farming communities the children help with the chores after school. The pace is slower. In real country playgrounds, with grass and trees, children play pretending games like Mothers and Fathers, and make huts. To take this to its farthest extreme, when I went up to Cape Wrath, the northwestern tip of Scotland, there were so few children, and in such far-flung homesteads, that there was no such thing as gathering together for a game—and the boys said that anyway they'd be too busy looking after the sheep.

LSM: Would you say something about how your methods of collecting information about children's games have evolved from the time you began work on *The Lore and Language of Schoolchildren* on through your more recent books?

IO: Actually the methods did not change much. We went on using the same rather long-winded method of sending informal questionnaires—just suggestions—to any teachers who were genuinely interested in the scheme. They got the children—right through the school—to answer our questions, and the results were sent to us in bulk, unsorted and uncorrected. Then we could ask individual children to explain or expand on some points. It was done on a very personal basis. We always found it best to do things the slow, old-fashioned way. Peter never even used a typewriter. So really the only innovation was when I started going to school playgrounds all over Great Britain with a tape recorder in the 1960s.

LSM: Just how widespread are the games you have studied?

IO: It would be safe to say that most of the basic games—skipping, for instance, and tops, marbles, fivestones, string figures, chasing and hiding games, singing games—are known in most countries of the world. There are a limited number of elements of games, and if a game seems to be new, it is likely to be a hybrid of elements. Elastic skipping seemed to be new—a loop of elastic is held round two people's ankles, you know, and the others take turns jumping the nearest strand over the other, and back again—but it is a mixture of a "higher and higher" game played with two parallel bamboo sticks, and the cat's cradle string game. Of course, it is well known that the games of skill—the tops, the kite flying—really belong to the Far East. European children are duffers in comparison. But that is probably because adults are still playing those games in the Far East, and the children have experts they can copy.

Tops have died out completely in Britain, though they were still going strong in places like Birmingham in the 1960s. There is a tinge of sadness when a game finally dies out, after centuries. I was happy to read in an article in *The New York Times* not long ago that some elderly people remembered playing the knife-throwing game of mumblety-peg in New York in their childhood in the 1920s. We never had it from old people, and we found it only out in the Hebrides, when we did our survey in the 1960s.

The older singing games—the courtship games—are undoubtedly dying out, and that is because their real function has gone. It seems silly to "stand and choose your lover" when you are only nine years old, and there are only girls in the ring—that is, in In and Out the Windows, once very popular in England and America. And the demise of the singing and dancing games was hastened when Cecil Sharp became frightened that they were dying out and thought he could save them by teaching them in schools. They were taken out of children's possession—their last owners—and became part of the curriculum.

LSM: You spoke before of the theatrical aspect of some children's games. There is also a theatrical quality to the *Alice* books, for instance when the narrator says in a sort of stage whisper: ". . . (for, you see, Alice had learnt several things of this sort in her lessons in the school room . . .)."

IO: I didn't like either of the *Alice* books when I was young because I felt all of this was an adult conspiracy. I hated books like A. E. Coppard's *Pink Furniture*. Some of those 1930s books were very whimsical. It was as if the author was trying to be "childlike." It embarrassed me terribly. I knew that he was high above me—you know, six feet tall, and I was only three or four feet tall—and that he was having fun in his way. I was not going to join in. I like straightforward action stories without any author coming into the book in his own adult persona whatsoever. A. A. Milne and Enid Bagnold in *Alice and Thomas and Jane* were all right, because the child part of their psyche was still intact.

LSM: That goes back to what you said a moment ago about adults interfering in children's games.

IO: Oh, yes. Children seethe with scorn for adults pretending to be children. Grown-ups joining in is quite unforgivable—playing Bears on the floor, crawling around pretending to be a bear. You just feel very sorry for them.

LSM: You have said that when you go to observe children in playgrounds, the children don't know quite what to make of you. You are not a teacher, and not a parent—and so they allow you to stay.

IO: Yes, and it is a great relief to me, as you've noticed, that I can't think of things on the spur of the moment. So I can't make suggestions to them about their games. I can only say: "Um." I say a lot of "Um's." "What on earth is that game you told me about last week? I've forgotten it already." So they come along. They're the teachers. A nice change for them, instead of being taught and stuffed with knowledge all the time. They are actually teaching me. All I have to be is my own genuine idiotic self and just record what they are saying and doing. One of the great things, I hope you'll agree, about our work is that we always like to use the children's own words because they are much more vivid and simple and get to the heart of the matter. Adult words are often cover-ups, people trying to be more impressive than they are by nature. A child would not mind saying: "That's a whatsit. We can't really explain, but we will show you."

LSM: The Finnish scholar of children's lore, Leea Virtanen, observed (in *Children's Lore*, Studia Fennica 22, Helsinki, 1978) a tendency of Finnish girls to be interested in playing what traditionally were considered boys' games. She found that the opposite phenomenon—boys playing girls' games—was not occurring. Her overall point was that such changes reflect changes in the larger society—in this case that of females trying on traditional male roles.

IO: There is always a swing backward and forward with the games. For instance, at the beginning of the nineteenth century, skipping rope was a boys' game. Little girls had skipping ropes, and they skipped very sedately in a graceful dancing way. Skipping ropes appear with young girls' fashions in some of the fashion plates, little ropes with red handles to match the little red shoes. But the actual long rope skipping, where you really exert yourself, was a boys' game. There are historical reasons for things changing, as well as some that are more mysterious. During the nineteenth century, British boys were trained in the Public Schools to be Empire-builders, and organized team sports were part of the training. At some point it became accepted that skipping was a girls' game. Since then, for a boy to join in skipping is to brand himself a sissy. All the boys do with skipping now is run through the ropes and irritate the girls, just teasing the girls. They run straight through their skipping games, pulling the rope out of their hands, causing an uproar. The girls turn around and spit at them like alley cats. But sometimes, as with singing games in a ring, which are now a female province, if it is a big enough craze, the boys will join in. And if all the boys join in, then there is no shame in it.

LSM: So it's different if just one boy wants to play?

IO: The only boy, yes. Anybody who is an odd man out, or odd girl out, is criticized. Girls who play marbles are branded tomboys, and any boy who joins in a game of A Big Ship Sails Through the Alley-Alley-O is known as effeminate. But there are some very strong-minded ones. There was one boy whom we saw in the middle of one of these games of A Big Ship Sails, and I asked him afterward about it, and he said: "I'm used to playing girls' games because I have five sisters, and I am not going to stop for anybody teasing me." He just thought that they were good games, and they are. They used to be for both sexes. They are mostly courtship games, or just for a whole village to enjoy in the evenings. During the Middle Ages, young adults used to play the games after dinner. One of the nicest experiences I ever had was in a school in Bedford, where they have a lot

Iona Opie

of immigrants from the West Indies, and the boys and girls were playing singing games together. It was thrilling to see the games played as they used to be, by young adults centuries ago—quite unselfconsciously—with a boy able to go into the ring and kiss a girl and change places without feeling awkward. They were more lively than British children as well, and they sang better—better diction, better pitch, better rhythm. Beautiful, they were.

LSM: You have written that children during the postwar years, when you began your researches, were more outgoing, freer about talking to an adult with notebook in hand, than the children of an earlier period might have been. Why do you think this?

IO: That's a rather large question. It has to do with the general loosening of social codes. Before the First World War, manners were formal, and everyone—not just children—was considerably in awe of their elders and betters. In the 1880s, when Lady Gomme and her correspondents were collecting games, a respectful hush would have descended on the village children if one of the gentry asked them what they were playing—and usually only the gentry had the leisure or interest to inquire. After the Second World War, the social strata more or less leveled out. There were many fewer servants to come between parents and children in middle-class homes. There was a new informality in the classroom—some people would say this has gone too far. The atmosphere was quite different.

LSM: Much has been written lately by sociologists and others about the growing sophistication of children, due to their exposure to television and so on. Have you noticed any decline in the age at which children feel they have outgrown certain games, any change that might tend to bear out these claims? What is your response to the proposition as a whole?

IO: It is very hard to say. Children were very sophisticated in the eighteenth century because parents got rid of them in those days by letting them spend most of their time in the servants' quarters, and the servants would be fairly outspoken, not very refined. So they would have learned all about the facts of life down with the servants. Some of the current "sophistication" is entirely on the surface—girls wearing earrings and high-heeled shoes. It has nothing to do with the way they think.

In one of my schoolyard reports, I say that the main activities in the school playground are eating crisps and playing Kiss Chase. They really seemed to be the most popular things for a long time. The children giggle and tease each other, and the boys try to embarrass the girls by playing a ring game like Shirley Temple: "I'm Shirley Temple, the girl with the curly hair . . ." And the girls pull up their skirts, and the boys all stand on the outside oohing and aahing and trying to annoy the girls. They know a lot of what goes on.

LSM: Some social critics have suggested that children are sophisticated today in the sense of being more consumer-oriented than formerly. I ask about this because it seems to me that the essence of game-playing is to do something for the fun of it, with no consequences that extend beyond the game, whereas a consumer is always concerned with what he will get back for his outlay.

IO: There is a certain amount of keeping up with the Joneses in the playground. It's rather pathetic sometimes, if a child comes from a poor family, and the other children have got the toys he sees on television. He feels inferior. Sometimes after Christmas a child will bring some very expensive toy to school, a transistor, or a special doll that talks.

LSM: Does that kind of competitiveness disrupt the whole playground?

IO: No. The children are very generous. The expensive doll will be lent all around. They take turns looking after it. I don't think this is a very important part of the playground community because the games go on, and the games are much more important than these objects. The children sit them down on a bench in a corner and go off and play the same old games. But there is a bit of keeping up with the Joneses.

LSM: The word "continuity" seems to be a key word in your books.

IO: Yes, that refers to the framework of the games, you see. The games are old, but they are always new to each generation of children. The children always think they made up the games themselves. At the beginning of the school year I am often buttonholed by some five-year-old: "Come and see our new game. Mandy has just made it up." And they go into a routine of skipping up and down with crossed arms: "Kitty and I went to tea / Lock the door and turn the key." It's a very old and rather ingenious game. They cross their arms—there are two little girls who cross arms, hold each other's hands, and magically when they get to the end of the playground, they can turn around without letting go of each other's hands. So that is new to them because they've only just learned it, and yet it has been going on for two hundred years or so. But I never disabuse them, because it's only a game.

LSM: I read that Kornei Chukovsky visited you once in England. What was he like?

IO: Oh, he was a marvelous man. He was a poet who had to become a children's poet because it was dangerous in the Soviet Union to be an adult poet anymore. We had been given various instructions about how to look after this eighty-four-year-old man. We were told that he liked to have a rest after lunch and couldn't stay very long because he got tired. Not a bit of it. This magnificent, tall, strong, energetic, talkative man arrived. He went up our staircase two steps at a time. "Ah, what are you going to show me?" He looked at our daughter's geography posters, was very interested in that. Then he started talking about how the authorities had shut him in the writers' village. "What are we supposed to do?" he said. "Go around showing each other our manuscripts?" He recited "The Crocodile" to us and then stopped in the middle and said: "But I'm busting, I'm busting!" (He meant "boasting.") He had come down with a young friend, and all the way back in their hired car they read nursery rhymes to each other. He was the epitome of the spirit of the nursery rhymes, the ebullience and the jollity and the vitality of them.

LSM: Why do you think that England has been such a rich source of nonsense?

IO: We pride ourselves on being eccentric. That's part of it. All the people in the nursery rhymes are definite characters, aren't they? They don't behave in a humdrum way at all, not in a respectable way. They keep eating each other!

> Robin the Bobbin, the big-bellied Ben,
> He ate more meat than fourscore men;
> He ate a cow, he ate a calf,
> He ate a butcher and a half,
> He ate a church, he ate a steeple,
> He ate the priest and all the people!

LSM: In the preface to *The Oxford Book of Children's Verse* (1973), you say that from seeing the poems gathered there in a chronological arrangement "we can appreciate more easily, perhaps, the shock that must have preceded glee when the Liddell children found their father's shy friend (Lewis Carroll) making fun of the poetry they had been brought up to learn and love; yet may remark how, despite Christ Church levity, Watts and Southey and the Taylors continued to be a part of children's normal repertoire at least to the end of the nineteenth century." What interests me is how a moralistic poem like Isaac Watts's "Against Idleness and Mischief" ("How doth the little busy bee . . .") and its parody can coexist in someone's mind. The parody, evidently, does not demolish the original altogether. Would you like to comment on this?

IO: I don't think they coexist, you have to choose one or the other—otherwise they contaminate each other. The Liddell children were delighted with the cleverness of Carroll's parodies—the sudden transformation into nonsense, and the parodies are what we know nowadays. We are scarcely aware of the originals. Yet Watts's "The Sluggard" is full of vivid images:

> 'Tis the voice of the sluggard: I heard him complain,
> "You have waked me too soon, I must slumber again."
> As the door on its hinges, so he on his bed
> Turns his sides and his shoulders and his heavy head.

I would choose that instead of Carroll's "'Tis the voice of the Lobster" any day. I just hope the parents of the late nineteenth century were wise enough to steer clear of the more obvious poems. I have to say that I am not a great appreciator of parody, myself, and—for different reasons—I wish Kingsley Amis had never thought of writing "Look thy last on all things shitty."

LSM: The *Alice* fantasies had their origin in a story that was first written down and illustrated as a homemade book for a particular child. Was the making of such one-of-a-kind gift books a relatively rare occurrence in nineteenth-century Britain, or was there a tradition of home bookmaking for children?

IO: Oh, yes, there was a lot of that. Very often it was a grandmother, or the proverbial maiden aunt who made them. We've got some in the Opie Collection, which is now at the Bodleian. A lot of them exist. Very often they used a traditional rhyme to base a book on and then elaborated. But often a story was woven around the children in a family, and then it was their book, and nobody else had a copy. In fact there was one such book in my family, the story of my cousin's children, *The Adventures of Jeannie and Gwen.*

Some families are tribal and have got their own name for people and objects. I know one family that calls their mother "Moth" and their dog "Dog" and their cat "Cat." The stepfather is "Pa Two." They say "ridilicus" instead of "ridiculous" because they like the sound better, and they call expensive cars "slooshy." They change words round to make them theirs.

LSM: That reminds me of what you said before about "heirloom rhymes." It's another illustration of family nonsense, nonsense as a tie that binds. In contrast to all that, children's book publishing has become an enormous industry. What trends have you noticed lately on the commercial side of bookmaking for the young?

IO: There are technical developments in color printing. They are always improving that. Bigger press runs have been made possible by the publishing of international editions. Children's books are more seriously regarded than they ever were before. I think we had a part in that because we started studying childish things. Now the study of childhood, children's books, and so forth has become an academic subject.

Children's book publishing is a much bigger business than it was before partly because parents are much more ambitious for their children. There is so much more opportunity now than there was before the war. And parents know that the key to all progress up the ladder for their children is learning to read.

LSM: There's progress again!

IO: Yes, that's right. We got back to that. But we're doing it through better channels now. More nonsense. More fun. Lovely alphabet books. And it's been recognized that there must be something in a children's book for the adult as well. Dr. Johnson once said to Mrs. Thrale, "Remember always that the parents buy the books and that the children never read them." About fifty years later William Godwin pointed out to Charles Lamb, "It is the children that read children's books, when they read, but it is the parents who choose them." At both those periods parents probably chose the books for the good effect they might be expected to have on their children. In the present day they are as likely to choose books for their younger children for the effect they may have on themselves: "Shall I enjoy reading this book aloud night after night? Is it well enough written to read aloud without my having to edit it as I go? Will I get bored with the story? Do I really like the pictures?" Only first-rate children's books—of which there are many nowadays—will satisfy the adult reader and the child listener alike.

....

Helen Oxenbury

Born June 2, 1938
Ipswich, England

H elen Oxenbury first made a name for herself as a scenic designer. By the time that her second child was born, she was finding it increasingly difficult, however, both to manage a home life and to work in the theater. Her husband, John Burningham, had already launched his career as a children's book author and artist. Following his example, Oxenbury turned to the picture book as an art form she might pursue at home. She published her first children's book, Numbers of Things, in 1967 and was the recipient three years later of the Kate Greenaway Medal, England's equivalent of the Caldecott Medal.

With the arrival of her third child, Oxenbury became interested in exploring the possibilities for books made with babies and toddlers specially in mind. The board books that followed were among the first to reach the newly emerging market of college-educated baby boomer parents who, by the 1980s, were eager to introduce their children to books from the earliest ages. Oxenbury's books in this genre have rarely been matched either for the overall quality of their design or for the refreshing realism of the comic touches with which she salted the works: babies spilling their juice and splattering their food, parents grimacing and panicking. A master watercolorist and draftsman, Oxenbury is also a canny psychologist who has managed, in all her books, to capture on paper the complex mix of emotions with which children and their parents respond to each other over the course of a day.

We taped this interview on November 6, 1989, at the offices of Margaret K. McElderry Books, New York, where Oxenbury was visiting in connection with the publication earlier that year of We're Going on a Bear Hunt (1989).

LEONARD S. MARCUS: What do babies see when they look at books? **HELEN OXENBURY:** They recognize faces and other babies, and all the little things they have around them—the dish that they eat out of and their high chair. It would be silly to do a board book with atmosphere and landscapes for a very, very tiny child who has no experience of that. All babies know is what happens in their home with their mom and dad. As an artist, one has to recognize what it is that children recognize.

LSM: What else goes into the making of books for the very young? **HO:** You have to consider that a board book is looked at with the parent. For the child, that's the best part—the parent saying: "Do you see the-this?" And: "Where is the-that?" So you must have a little bit of something in the book that the mother or father will recognize and laugh about, so that they don't think: Oh God, I just can't take that book and look at it again!

LSM: You've given the baby on the cover of Working (1981) a faceful of food.

HO: Exactly. That's something we all know about, isn't it? Relationships between the child and other members of the family, or friends, can also be brought into the pictures of a board book. By the end of Dressing (1981), the baby is dressed and ready to go, and it's implied that a parent is on the scene lending a hand, even though I haven't actually shown that in the pictures.

LSM: In many board books—but not in yours—babies are always smiling.

HO: When babies are eating or on the pot, they don't smile, because they're concentrating on something else. In making books, what I try to show is how things really are.

LSM: Are there other ways in which your experience as a parent has helped shape your work?

HO: When our first two children were babies, we didn't think that they would even want to look at books. But Emily, our third one, suffered as a child from eczema. To stop her scratching we used to walk up and down with her until we almost fell over, and we used to show her magazines. We were absolutely amazed when she began to point things out at a very young age, before she was one, certainly. And you know how one has catalogs of children's clothes, things like that? She used to look and laugh at and enjoy them. So for this little girl who had eczema, I went specially to the store to look for board books with very simple drawings of things—and there really wasn't much at all available. That's when I began to make my own.

LSM: In your most recent board book series (*Clap Hands* [1987], etc.), you have drawn four babies, each of a different racial group. Do very young children identify with the characters in their books on that level?

HO: I think it probably doesn't matter a damn to them. They only start noticing when they pick up ideas about race and ethnicity from their parents. But there weren't any board books that had a multiracial feel to them, so I thought: Why shouldn't there be? Because that's how the world is. I tried to do it very unselfconsciously.

LSM: Your *Out-and-About* books (*The Birthday Party* [1983], *Eating*

Out [1983], etc.) are for children who have just outgrown board books. What do the books of that series have in common?

HO: They're concerned with those quite traumatic little events in a child's life, such as the first day of school or a birthday party.

LSM: In *The Birthday Party,* one little girl guest doesn't want to surrender her present to the birthday boy who, in turn, is much more interested in his gifts than his guests.

HO: Again, we've all been through those experiences. And the parent looking on is thinking: Better say thank you, and the child doesn't, of course. Children just want to know what's coming next. Adults, you see, put children in very trying situations and expect them to perform and behave. Adults love to go for a trip in the car, look at the countryside, and go and have tea. But for a child, to be strapped in the back of the car is the most boring thing in the world. So you can't blame the child in *The Car Trip* (1983) when all he thinks about is teasing the dog and . . . I forget what else happens. . . .

LSM: He throws up.

HO: Oh, yes! He's had too much to eat because eating is all he can do, sitting in the back of the car. *Eating Out* is about the fact that young children loathe going to restaurants. They'd much rather be at home. But I'm not so much saying in that book that the poor parents shouldn't go out to eat. Why shouldn't they? The point is that they're not the only ones who have a child who can't bear it. I think when children misbehave, parents think that they're the only ones who've got a child who does this sort of thing. Of course, everybody's child does.

LSM: By the same token, children often believe that the things they're afraid of, or can't stand, or aren't good at, are unique to themselves. Your books also show them that that isn't so.

HO: That's right. At the same time, though, I'm quite suspicious of books that set out to teach things. A picture book, after all, is primarily a stepping-stone to reading. That is what one hopes will happen in the end. What a book must do is to make a child want to read it, to make him think: Oh, gosh, now what's going to happen?—and turn the page.

LSM: As a child, did you have books that affected you that strongly?

HO: I was a baby during the war, when very few books were available. I had a large book of Shirley Temple photographs, which I absolutely loved, though I can see now it was pretty dreadful.

LSM: It's surprising sometimes, isn't it, what books children actually like?

HO: Oh, yes. My brother and I also had some of the classics, Kenneth Grahame's *The Wind in the Willows*, Beatrix Potter's *The Tale of Peter Rabbit*.

LSM: *Peter Rabbit*, like your own work, is for the younger ages. Why do you think it has become a "classic"?

HO: It's a very good adventure story. Things happen and all the emotions become involved. It starts off with a safe sort of family situation. The mother goes off shopping and tells the children to be good. But there's the one little rebel, Peter, who does the very thing he's been told not to do, he goes into Mr. MacGregor's garden. I'm sure children identify with Peter. So a slight sort of tension builds, because you know he shouldn't be there and because something's looming. Then he's seen, and there's the great chase, and you feel very sorry for poor old Peter Rabbit as he gets caught up in the netting. Then comes the relief at the end when he escapes. It's not a morality tale, just good earthy naughtiness.

LSM: Were you interested in visual things as a child?

HO: I can't remember a time when I didn't draw and paint. My father, who was an architect, did quite a few little pictures for my brother and me. There was one lovely painting of a community of elves living in the roots of a tree which overhung a river. I shall never forget that.

LSM: Have childhood memories played a part in your own books?

HO: The muddy estuary in *We're Going on a Bear Hunt* is very much based on a place where I played as a child. My illustrations for that book also express, I think, the freedom I felt to go out into the country on my own or with a crowd of other children—which children don't have now. You don't dare let children go around on their own, especially in London.

LSM: It's curious, then, that you included a parent in the scenes where the children have gone off hunting for bear. Is it a sign of our times—of children needing to be protected—that you did so?

HO: I don't know. Hmmm. The stories I loved as a child were actually the ones where there weren't any adults around—adventure stories with children who just coped on their own.

What I quite like about the *Bear Hunt* book is that the text allows the illustrations to do as much work as the words themselves. For instance, in the line, "We're going on a bear hunt," the "we" is never described. We're never told who "we" are, so it is entirely up to the illustrator to create the characters. The scenes with the snowstorm and the mud are also never described, so again it was up to me to decide how they looked. Then the bear: we're not told what sort of bear it is, whether fierce or friendly. The text has a wonderful way of gathering speed, so I had to find a way of not letting the illustrations slow it down. That's why it becomes like a strip cartoon toward the end as the family rush back home with the bear at their heels. At the very end, I made the bear look a bit lonely, as though he would have liked to have played with those kids, who instead have run away from him. You know: "Wait for me! Come out and play!"

LSM: These days, publishers—and many parents—seem to think that the more color there is in a picture book, the better. Why do you often choose to alternate black-and-white illustrations with color ones?

HO: I had to slightly fight for that in the *Bear Hunt* book. I can remember books with black-and-white illustrations that I loved as a child. Suddenly, when you knew you were coming to a color picture, there would be the excitement of turning the page, and finally there it was. It's the contrast that's so dramatic, I suppose.

LSM: In your books you often show parents in off-guard moments: a tired father with his feet up on the sofa, a mother half-dressed in a department store dressing room. Why is that?

HO: It's almost the opposite of a television commercial, where everything is perfect, and the mother produces white clothes out of the washing machine. I find that awful because it's not true, and because it makes people dissatisfied and feel inadequate.

In *We're Going on a Bear Hunt,* when the bear is finally found, it's the dad who runs like hell to get away, ahead of the children, which of course is meant to be comical. I think it's very important to show the child that parents are only human. To show that they have weaknesses is perhaps not a bad thing.

LSM: In your drawings you'll sometimes include a discarded bottle or an old tire floating in the river or lying in a lot. Why do you think such details might interest children?

HO: I can remember having more fun as a child throwing stones at a tin can on the beach than from playing with any expensive toy. Our own children don't seem to want all the toys that are available. Some parents have a desperate feeling that they're not good parents if they don't buy all those expensive toys.

LSM: Why is that?

HO: There's a desire to fill every moment of the child's life—with lessons, toys, after-school activities. As a result, many children have lost the ability to be quiet and entertain themselves with fantasy games of their own devising. At least, there's a tendency for this to happen.

LSM: The *Tom and Pippo* books are about just such fantasy games, aren't they?

HO: That's right. Little Tom doesn't have great expensive toys. He just has his friend Pippo.

LSM: Are those books based on personal experience?

HO: Tom I suppose is my son when he was a little lad. Pippo was his dog, a real dog, not a doll. The two of them were pretty inseparable, and the dog used to get blamed for an awful lot of things. Of course, we knew what was going on.

LSM: The stories are told in the first person, in Tom's voice. So when a parent is reading aloud to a child, the parent . . .

HO: . . . becomes the "I." That's right.

LSM: That gives the parent a chance to see things from the child's point of view.

HO: It was because of the warmth of the "I" that I eventually came round to writing stories that way. I used to visit schools a lot and sometimes a class of little children would have written their own *Tom and Pippo* story.

LSM: Were their stories very different from your own?

HO: They were usually very, very similar, to the point where you knew they'd probably had a jolly good look . . .

LSM: Well, Tom is quite a mimic himself: Tom's father reads, so Tom wants to read, and so on.

HO: Yes, and then Tom becomes the father to the monkey.

LSM: That type of role reversal must be one of the most basic kinds of children's play.

HO: It's a testing, isn't it, a testing things out.

LSM: In your books it also becomes comical.

HO: One of the most important things is to laugh with your children and to let them see you think they're being funny when they're trying to be. It gives children enormous pleasure to think they've made you laugh. They feel they've reached one of the nicest parts in you. Tom makes a dreadful mess and says, "It was him. It was the monkey." As a picture book artist, I don't think one can be too much on the side of the child.

....

Jerry Pinkney

Born December 22, 1939
Philadelphia, Pennsylvania

....

Old-fashioned storytelling played an important part in Jerry Pinkney's World War II–era Philadelphia childhood. Grown-ups in his all-black neighborhood told each other, as much for their own entertainment as for the children's, time-honored tales about Brer Rabbit, Brer Fox, and John Henry. As a child, Pinkney was among the rapt listeners; as an illustrator, he has enjoyed the chance to help pass down these and other traditional African-American folk stories to new generations.

Pinkney became a children's book illustrator in the 1960s while continuing to work in the commercial art arena for which he had trained. Influenced by the Civil Rights movement, publishers at that time were starting to address their past failure to champion black authors and illustrators for children and to publish books that more accurately reflected the multiracial nature of American society. For Pinkney, this historic change opened up unprecedented opportunities. In the years that followed, he illustrated books for young readers by Verna Aardema, Mildred D. Taylor, Patricia C. McKissack, Virginia Hamilton, Eloise Greenfield, and his most frequent collaborator, Julius Lester.

If there was a dilemma for Pinkney in the growing demand for picture *books celebrating African-American themes, it lay in his eagerness not to become known soley as an illustrator working in that—or in any one— vein. It was in part for this reason that he chose to illustrate* The Little Match Girl *(1999) and* The Ugly Duckling *(1999), Hans Christian Andersen stories his mother had read to him as a child. When we recorded this interview in his suburban New York studio on October 27, 1999, Pinkney was in the midst of gathering reference material for a new edition of* Aesop's Fables *(2000).*

LEONARD S. MARCUS: What is it about watercolor that appeals to you as the medium for so much of your work?

JERRY PINKNEY: My first passion is drawing. I have always loved the energy and spontaneity of drawing. And so it was fine with me that when I began to illustrate books in the 1960s, full-color printing was considered too costly for children's books, and I was limited to doing line art, with perhaps two or three additional colors that had to be preseparated. I thought of the lines of my drawings for those first books as holding lines for the color. Then in the mid-1980s, full color became available for use in children's trade books, and combining watercolor with drawing seemed a natural way to keep the sense of energy and spontaneity in the work. *The Patchwork Quilt* (1985) is the first picture book for which I worked in this way.

Watercolor allows me to bring a certain freshness to a drawing that, in reality, had to be very carefully thought out and planned. I enjoy the translucent quality, the fact that when the paper shows through you get a sense of light. That is kind of magical for me. That sense of surface, of the paper playing a role in the look and feel of the picture, is, I think, a good part of what attracts artists to watercolor and why people enjoy looking at watercolor art. It allows the

Jerry Pinkney •

viewer, in a sense, to step into the picture, to finish the picture by seeing it with their mind's eye.\

LSM: You often let your pencil lines show through.

JP: Every project starts with a strong line drawing. If I want the book to look more painterly, then I keep painting over the line and eventually the line will soften and begin to disappear. Now if I want the line to play a part in the energy of the book, I'll go back over the line. Sometimes I will leave lines from a drawing that I have worked over in order to let the viewer see something of how the picture developed. That is another way of giving immediacy to the work.

LSM: When did you begin to draw?

JP: I remember always drawing. At first, I drew anything with wheels. Later, when I was eleven, I got my first job, working at a newspaper stand, and would take a pad and pencil with me and draw the people I saw waiting for the bus or trolley. I would also draw the window displays at the department store that was across from my newsstand. By then I was drawing whatever I saw around me.

LSM: Did your parents encourage your interest in art?

JP: My mother always praised my drawings and my father, who painted houses and was a jack-of-all-trades, used to tack white wall-paper on the walls of our bedroom so that I could draw directly on the wall while lying in bed! Although my father did not encourage me as directly as did my mother, there was a certain encouragement implied in his making sure that if I wanted to doodle, I would have something to doodle on. From a very early age I would go off with him to help with his work, and whenever we went into Newton's paint store to buy house paint, there would always be the moment when I walked past the aisle with art supplies. Somehow, just in seeing the brushes and pads, I found a kind of encouragement.

LSM: Was your father also a woodworker? You show wood-grain patterns in so many of your illustrations. It seems to be a subject for which you have a special feeling.

JP: Yes, he did. Woodworking was one of the things my father did quite a bit of, especially toward the end of his life. He was very proud of how he could refinish furniture. He knew about wood grain and mastered a variety of techniques. Now I find that I can endlessly draw the patterns of wood grains and never find it boring.

LSM: Were books important to you as a child?

JP: I'm dyslexic, so as a child I struggled with reading. I avoided anything with words. Unlike many artists of my generation, I did not even read comic books, and I did not draw from comic books, either. My interest in books came much later in life, through the vehicle of drawing and my appreciation of storytelling in art.

My mother was a big reader, and my sister recalls that she often read us fairy tales, including the stories of Hans Christian Andersen. She also read the Bible and the essays of Ralph Waldo Emerson, and I can recall that as a teenager, despite the fact that I had such trouble reading even simple books, I took up Emerson myself. I had to struggle with him, but I had become so fascinated with his sense of nature and universal balance. Looking back, it seems paradoxical that I would have shied away from comic books but not from Emerson.

I remember *The Story of Little Black Sambo* as the only book from my childhood in which I saw a depiction of a child of color. I liked the book for that reason, as well as for the fantasy of the story. Our family owned a copy, and my parents, who were very proud people, must have thought it good, because they would not have had a book in the house that had to be explained away or that in any way undercut their strong sense of self.

LSM: Do you have childhood memories of World War II?

JP: I remember the large-formatted photojournalistic magazines,

Jerry Pinkney •

Life and *Look*. We had a wardrobe in the upstairs hall at home, and it was in that wardrobe that my mother and father kept copies of the magazines, because they did not want us children to see photographs of the war. But often when I was home alone, I would go to the wardrobe, take out the magazines, and lie mesmerized on the second-floor landing, looking at them. I remember the powerful impact that those large photographic images had on me, and remember the horror portrayed in some of them, especially those of the concentration camps taken at the end of the war. My parents never talked about the war with me, so the pictures spoke volumes.

LSM: Tell me about meeting John J. Liney. You dedicated *The Hired Hand* (1997), which is the story of a younger person's apprenticeship to a master, to him.

JP: John Liney, who drew a well-known comic strip called *Little Henry*, lived in Philadelphia. Having noticed me drawing at my newsstand one day, he introduced himself to me and invited me to visit his studio. Meeting John Liney was a milestone—in ways I did not fully realize right away. By the time we met I had somehow already gotten the idea that drawing was a noble activity, and I remember thinking then that I had nobler things to do as an artist than to draw cartoons. Yet it made an incredible impression on me just to see that he sat down every day at a drawing board, surrounded by all sorts of wonderful art materials, and made his living by drawing and was happy doing it. I visited his studio several times. He was an older man, and although for that reason I did not think of him as a friend, we really were friends.

LSM: Philadelphia has a long history as a center of the visual arts. Charles Willson Peale, Thomas Eakins, Howard Pyle, Jesse Willcox Smith, Maxfield Parrish, John Sloan, and others lived there. Did you become aware of that history during the time you were growing up in the city?

JP: I did not become aware of that until much later. About ten years ago I became very interested in the Ashcan School painters and was surprised to learn that half of those guys came from Philadelphia. I never entered an art museum or gallery until I was in college.

LSM: What about Philadelphia's historic role during the American Revolution and in the early years of the republic? Were you taught to feel proud of the city's heritage while growing up?

JP: Germantown, where we lived, was quite a distance from the center of the city. We would have had to travel to get there. And I'm not sure whether parts of Philadelphia at that time were not segregated, or at least that the impression was given that they were segregated. Certainly there were places that we as black people did not go. So, no, when I was growing up we did not participate in that sense of the grandeur of Philadelphia's history. When I go to Philadelphia now, I do so because of the city's history and rich cultural life. It sometimes feels like a makeup course for all the things I missed out on as a child.

LSM: Did you experience other forms of racial discrimination while growing up?

JP: It was more something that I was aware of rather than something I experienced myself. But in senior year in high school, an instructor who had always been very fair in his grading made it clear that he did not think it best for the black students to continue on to college to study art, because there would be no future for us. In his own mind, he may have thought he was doing us a favor.

LSM: But you ignored his advice.

JP: Yes, I did. At the Philadelphia College of Art, I majored in graphic design—the practical side of art—in part because my father was skeptical about the possibility of making a living as a fine artist. I was probably unsure about this myself. I thought that if I had a degree in design, I would always be able to find some entry-level job

Jerry Pinkney

after graduation. The illustration department was located on the floor above ours and the interesting thing was that they and we were two completely different cultures—different in the way we dressed, the way we spoke—everything. When no one was up there, however, I would go up to see what was hanging on the walls. I remember being very impressed. The illustration students worked in the tradition of Howard Pyle and N. C. Wyeth, but things were changing. Milton Glaser, Seymour Chwast, and the other members of Push Pin Studio in New York were looking at design and illustration as interrelated, and their ideas were affecting the way everyone viewed their work. So, as an experiment, the illustration department and the design department at my school decided to get together and exchange projects. Each department came up with a project for the other department to do. That assignment gave me a chance to think more about illustration, which I was already mildly interested in.

LSM: As an art student, did you also bump up against Abstract Expressionism as a force to be reckoned with?

JP: Oh, yes! In high school my training had all been practical: How to render products; how to use an airbrush; how to do calligraphy. When I got to college one of my painting instructors said to me, "I'm going to break you yet!" I was doing realistic painting, because that is what I had been taught. But to painters of that time, Abstract Expressionism was it. So it all just hit me—Boom! I began to paint in that manner myself and continued to do so for years. I think that if I were to go back to painting, I would paint abstractions again. In fact, if you look at my illustration work in an abstract way, just look at the backgrounds, the foliage and tree trunks, and move away from the figures, you'll see that interest in abstraction expressing itself.

LSM: When did you leave Philadelphia?

JP: I married, started a family, and left art school after two and a half years. We moved up to Boston, where I went to work for the Rust-craft greeting card company. Boston had a strong design community and a strong painting community. I felt a need at that time to be around other African-American artists, and from that standpoint as well, Boston was a good place to be. I became somewhat active in the Civil Rights movement—involved with voter registration and community group meetings, and with organizing pressure on large companies to hire African-Americans—and found those experiences energizing.

Boston, of course, was also a publishing center, and when I later went to work for a design firm called Barker-Black, I was assigned to illustrate a book project that they had under contract. During the sixties, publishers were interested in publishing African-American material and were eager to hire black illustrators. So the opportunities were there, and I found that as a book illustrator I could combine my design training in problem-solving with my passion for drawing. It was amazing. Everything fell into place.

LSM: Were you looking at picture books with your children at home? Did the books you became acquainted with have an impact on the direction of your own work?

JP: I'm sure I noticed how hard it was to find a book with black children as characters. That must have had an impact on me. We looked for such books for our children. And I can remember when Ezra Jack Keats's *The Snowy Day* was published in 1962. I understood the impact of *The Snowy Day*, but I didn't see it at the time as an example of a kind of book that I could imagine myself doing. I began by illustrating African folktales and then went on to illustrate folktales from other cultures. I did not yet see myself as an artist who might one day illustrate a contemporary story such as *The Patchwork*

Jerry Pinkney

Quilt. In any case, I still thought of editorial illustration, rather than book illustration, as my idea of a noble calling and as the thing I most wanted to do.

I continued to do books because of the satisfaction I took in creating a well-made object that I could hold in hand. Later, my awareness of the need for books on African-American subjects, interpreted positively, became a second reason. I began to feel that through such books I could make a contribution to society.

The Boston and New York art communities were two separate communities. I began to feel that I wanted to be in New York, that I would find a wider range of opportunities there. And so in 1970, my family and I moved to New York.

LSM: Were you still doing advertising and editorial illustration?

JP: Yes, that work provided me with most of my income.

LSM: Tell me about the Seagram's black history calendars you designed in the 1970s.

JP: When large corporations began to see that minorities represented a potential market, they began setting up departments to figure out how to target that market. I think they genuinely also wanted to make a constructive contribution of some kind. Seagram's decided to commission a series of black history calendars. I did four calendars, including one called "The Black West," for which my wife, Gloria Jean, wrote the legends. I loved doing those calendars. I started collecting history books around that time, and it was also then that I became acquainted with the New York Public Library's Schomburg Center for Research in Black Culture.

LSM: When did book illustration finally become the main focus of your work?

JP: It was not until around the time that I illustrated *Mirandy and Brother Wind* (1988) that I reorganized my work life. After accepting a teaching position at the University of Delaware, I told my agent for commercial work that I wanted to take some time off to concentrate more on illustrating books.

Mirandy marks the point in my career where I was beginning to do more intensive research and to associate research with a sense of discovery. I no longer felt I was just illustrating a book. I was *in* the book and beginning to create storytelling through pictures. I was learning about a part of my culture that I did not know about and using that learning experience as fuel for the art.

LSM: So you came to enjoy research.

JP: I love research. The Schomburg used to be my main source of material, but by now I have put together my own extensive files on the Underground Railroad, the slave trade, plantation life, and the like. If I run into some detail for which I lack specific information, as I did while working on *Minty* (1996), for example, I just call a friend who is the curator of costumes and furniture at the National Park Service. He is able to supply me with whatever I need.

LSM: Why did you dedicate *John Henry* (1994) to your father?

JP: I did so because in some ways my father was a heroic man to me. He was a very independent man. At an early age he decided to work for himself. I think he really thought he was the strongest person in the world! We would always have a conversation about whether he should have an aluminum ladder instead of the monstrous wooden one that he liked to use, and always he would refuse to change. For him it was: the heavier the better.

I grew up with the story of John Henry and know that I must have been impressed by the image of a black man beating a steam drill. And so, when my agent and I were talking one day about new projects, *John Henry* came to mind. The public domain retellings I found were not very good. They were stereotypical—and vicious in a way. My editor at Dial, Phyllis Fogelman, and I asked Julius Lester, whose

Jerry Pinkney

four volumes of *Uncle Remus* retellings I had already illustrated, if he would write the text.

Julius and I had met only once or twice at conference book signings and had not been in direct contact with each other during the time I was illustrating the *Uncle Remus* collections. But when we proposed the *John Henry* project to him, he called me wanting to know what was my interest in John Henry. He said he had not thought much about the story and wasn't particularly interested in it. I told him about my childhood memories of having heard the story at home. As we continued to talk, he began to relate John Henry to Dr. Martin Luther King Jr. That association, he said, would be his inspiration.

Like *Mirandy*, *John Henry* was a turning point for me, in that I was able to create illustrations that parallel the text without mimicking it, and to add my own pictorial story lines. One reason that I love working with Julius is that he inspires visual images other than the ones he's actually describing. In the opening scene, Julius writes about the animals all coming out of the forest to see the young baby. This gave me the idea to have the animals follow John Henry all throughout the book. In the spread where a boulder is being dynamited, for instance, I show John Henry holding back two burros, even though the animals aren't mentioned in the text. But I knew that burros would have been needed to carry materials to the work site and that they would have bolted at the sound of the dynamite blast. So this became another way to show John Henry's incredible strength.

The art is much more developed in *John Henry* than in earlier books. There are a great many characters in the pictures, and they're always active in some way. Instead of having the drawing lines play the dominant role, I brought more depth to the watercolor, with the result that edges define forms as well as the line. It takes a lot longer to paint that way.

LSM: I wondered about that look of solidity. Was it because John Henry is a mythic figure that you wanted to make him appear more securely anchored in the real world?

JP: Well, that's part of it. That's the intuitive part of my working process. I'll have a certain vision for the way a story should look. You'll notice that John Henry always breaks the planes of the book. I wanted him to be too big for the book to contain. That was part of my vision, too.

LSM: Tell me about your interest in drawing animals, which you have done across a wide spectrum, from naturalistic to personified.

JP: Before doing the first book of *Uncle Remus* tales, I had been illustrating a story retold by Verna Aardema called *Rabbit Makes a Monkey of Lion* (1989), for which I did not want to render the animals either naturalistically or in a fully anthropomorphic style. When I came to do the *Uncle Remus* tales, I first tried to do the illustrations in the same manner as *Rabbit* but saw they weren't working. I finally resolved the problem by posing for the animals myself. I had Polaroids taken of me acting out the different animal parts.

I have a great interest in and sense of wonder at animal life. Sometimes I show the qualities I see in the animals themselves. But Arthur Rackham, with his fantastic approach to the natural world, has also been an inspiration to me.

LSM: Tell me more about your working relationship with Julius Lester.

JP: By the time I met Julius, at a conference where we were signing for the *Uncle Remus* tales, I felt I already knew him through his novels and autobiography. There is a connection between us. We're the same age. He grew up in the South and I grew up in the North, and

I have been able to learn a lot from Julius about how someone who is black and from the South might respond to a particular situation. He has helped me to understand some aspects of segregation and prejudice that I saw mainly in historical terms but had not been able to relate to personally. For instance, I thought of Uncle Remus as a symbol of stability, as one of the older wise people of the community. I wanted to show Uncle Remus as a figure of strength. Julius did not want me to depict him at all. He wanted the reader to become the teller of the tales. He also preferred the characters not be playing the banjo. I love the look of the instrument, but it can be viewed as stereotypical.

LSM: Would you agree that African-American children's books have now entered the mainstream?

JP: Yes, I would. The books are no longer just sold in stores in a special "African-American" section, and I think that large numbers of books are being purchased by non-African-American parents for their children. I would love to see us get to the point where, in the literature that speaks to the history of and contributions to the field of children's literature, we no longer find African-American children's book artists discussed chiefly in the multicultural section. It would be a great leap if artists such as myself could be talked about more, not only in relation to our subject but simply in terms of our work as artists and storytellers.

Julius and I talk a lot about what we would like to see in children's books with an African-American subject, how we might possibly be able to enlarge on what is available. We find a lot of historical books being published, and lots of remembrances, but we don't often find fantasy. We also look for areas we share the same excitement about. I was aware of Julius's interest in the West, and so I sent him a copy of the Seagram's black history calendar. He remembered the story from his collection *Long Journeys Home: Stories from Black History* (1972) called "The Man Who Was a Horse" and decided to rewrite it as a picture book, *Black Cowboy, Wild Horses* (1998). One of the things we talked about then was myth, the fact that myths take a long time to create, but that you have to start somewhere. So we took the true story of the life of Bob Lemmons and tried to make him into a mythical character, which is basically the way Americans think of the West anyway. So each project that we've done starts with a shared vision. That's what cements the collaboration and makes it very balanced. Because we're both energized by the subject itself, we're better able to listen to each other.

In the case of *Black Cowboy, Wild Horses*, Julius had wanted the book to be very quiet and to simply deal with the man and his horse and nature and the wild mustangs. Whereas for me as a visual story-teller, even though I loved the story as he wrote it, I didn't find enough to work with visually to make the book exciting. So Julius and I spent a day together, discussing the possibilities of bringing more action or more tension to the book. He listened to my ideas, we brainstormed, and Julius gave me what I needed.

LSM: Why did you want to reillustrate *The Story of Little Black Sambo* as *Sam and the Tigers* (1996)?

JP: First of all, because it is a book I remembered from childhood. While doing some research at the Charles L. Blockson Afro-American Collection at Temple University, my wife, Gloria Jean, spotted a shelf with other illustrated versions of *Little Black Sambo* and with other books written by Helen Bannerman. I began to think that if there had been more than one version, there could be another version, too. Research showed there were over fifty versions. It seemed to me that during the 1950s and '60s, *Little Black Sambo* became somewhat frozen as a symbol of insensitivity toward children of color. People still referred to it as that, and I realized that it would always be that way unless someone brought about a change.

LSM: How did you come to do *Journeys with Elijah* (1999)?

JP: One of the things I have been trying to do of late is to speak of and celebrate not only my own culture but other cultures as well. That is the direction in which I want my work to go. Recognizing other peoples' differences in terms of culture or race is one of the ways that we can come to terms with and celebrate the world. So here was a manuscript that dealt with the worldwide migration of the Jews, and with the message of the prophet Elijah, and that was also a collection of eight folktales from seven countries and several historical periods. I saw illustrating this book as an opportunity to express my interest in different cultures and to learn more about other peoples and cultures in the process. That is the part of my work that I find especially rewarding, because it's what you don't know that can become an open door to understanding.

·················

Maurice Sendak

Born June 10, 1928
Brooklyn, New York

....

© Chris Callis

M*aurice Sendak, the children's book world's preeminent artist, began his career in the early 1950s, at a time when young children were typically depicted in books as angelic-looking, carefree, and blond. These idealized images were a far cry from the scrappy, unbeautiful, daydreamy youngsters Sendak had grown up with in tenement Brooklyn, and had himself been sketching since childhood. The "Sendak kids," who first made their appearance* in print in such early books as A Hole Is to Dig (1952) *and* A Very Special House *(1953), had fun, all right, but they also got angry, lonely, and bored. Insisting that young children wanted—even needed—to see a broader range of their own emotional experiences reflected in books, Sendak did more than anyone to free the picture book from its sentimental past.*

By the time Sendak won the 1964 Caldecott Medal for Where the Wild Things Are *(1963), he was already the recipient of five Caldecott Honors and the illustrator of more than fifty books, of which he was also the author of seven. His maverick approach sometimes stirred up controversy, but few critics disputed the sheer artistry of his illustrations. As his work was exhibited at museums around the world and adapted for the stage, film, and television, Sendak came to play a pivotal role in raising the status and appreciation level of children's books and their illustration generally.*

A largely self-taught artist, Sendak was nurtured during much of his career by the legendary editor Ursula Nordstrom. More recently, he assumed the mentor's role as the cofounder and director of the Night Kitchen Children's Theater and as an increasingly active presence in the worlds of opera, dance, television, and film.

When we recorded the first of these two interviews at the artist's Connecticut home on July 7, 1988, Sendak was absorbed in overseeing the printing of Dear Mili *(1988). We taped the second interview by telephone on June 14, 1993, in advance of the publication that year of* We Are All in the Dumps with Jack and Guy *(1993).*

INTERVIEW I: JULY 8, 1988

LEONARD S. MARCUS: Once when you were ill as a child, your father told you that if you looked out the window without blinking you might see an angel. In many of your children's books, characters stare out at the reader. Are they, too, looking for angels?

MAURICE SENDAK: I remember that incident clearly, as if it were yesterday. It hurts not to blink, and I didn't blink until my eyes watered, but I did see an angel. And when I saw him or her or it go by, I screamed and my father came rushing in. And, of course, in *Where the Wild Things Are*, Max doesn't blink once.

LSM: You have said that it is your ability to recall the "emotional quality of particular moments in childhood" that distinguishes you as a children's book illustrator. Yet at various times in the past you have also dismissed your work for children as secondary and said that you wished there was no real notion of children's books per se. Do you still feel that way?

MS: No. I think part of the reason I felt that way was due to resentment; the establishment critics looked contemptuously, or at the very least patronizingly, on the art in children's books. Now that I have spent nearly ten years in the theater and have gotten to be sixty years old, that resentment has dissipated. I like being a children's illustrator; I'd rather be one. Children are the best living audience in the world because they are so thoroughly honest. "Dear Mr. Sendak, I love your book. Marry me. Yours truly." "Dear Mr. Sendak, I hate your book. Die soon. Cordially." How could you not love those responses?

LSM: Do you get many letters from children about your books?

MS: Predominantly I get form letters. "Our teacher said we should write to our favorite author. We like your book *Where the Wild Things Are* very much. Where does Max go? When does he come back? Will you send us a free copy of the book, a photograph of yourself, a vial of your blood, your left ear. . . ." Sadly, very few letters come directly from children.

LSM: *Where the Wild Things Are* remains the book you are best known for, notwithstanding the theater work and the many other books you've done over the years. How do you feel about that?

MS: Well, that isn't entirely true, but it is to a large degree. It is not my favorite book, but it is a book I'm extremely fond of and very proud of. It's fine if that's the one I'm going to be known by.

Originally, *Wild Things* came out in spirals of scandal. People said it was too frightening, too ugly, that it wasn't a children's book, and so on. Bruno Bettelheim denounced it on the grounds that it would keep children up, was frightening. He also didn't like that Max was denied food. He did come round to agreeing with me years later. But his initial reactions did me a disservice. It was a very peculiar book for children back in the sixties.

LSM: And yet a committee of librarians got together when the book was still quite new and awarded it the Caldecott Medal.

Maurice Sendak

MS: I think that is probably the most astonishing fact of my entire life. I was thirty-four. I had already been in the business since I was eighteen and had been a runner-up for the award five times previous to that. The Caldecott Medal helped sell the book, but it also helped give me the power to continue to do the kind of books I wanted to do. It didn't make me feel that I could do even more outrageous books, because I didn't think my books were outrageous. The fact that other people did has always been a puzzle to me.

LSM: Over the course of the book, the pictures change in size, and eventually the pictures displace the words altogether. Is that meant to reflect Max's development in the story?

MS: Well, it's based on a theory of picture book making that I suppose I evolved myself, since I never took a course in bookmaking. It's a theory based on the work of artists I love, primarily Randolph Caldecott, Jean de Brunhoff (creator of the *Babar* books), and William Nicholson (whose masterpiece was *Clever Bill*). That device is a way of dramatically picturing what's going on; as Max's rage engorges him, those pictures fill the page. When his anger turns to a kind of wild jungle pleasure, the words are pushed off the page altogether. And then he deflates like any normal child; he's getting hungry, he's getting tired, and he wants to go back home.

LSM: In your new book, Wilhelm Grimm's tale *Dear Mili*, two of the last pages are all text. As Mili and her mother are reunited, it's the pictures that have been pushed off the page.

MS: It's the same reasoning in reverse; there is no time for pictures there, the music of Grimm's prose takes over. It would be an irritant to see what is being said at that point, so I let people read it and enjoy the music and the imagery; they don't need me to draw it for them. The illustrator must have more respect for language than he has for picture making; he must assume the backseat.

LSM: How did the Wild Things dolls come about, and how did you feel about turning your characters into toys?

MS: I'd always wanted the toys because I'm a toymaker, or was, with my brother Jack. I helped design the Wild Things dolls, basing their proportions on the early Mickey Mouse doll, which I adored.

LSM: The majority of your children's book characters have been boys—boys whose names begin with M and who bear a striking resemblance to you as a child. From what you have observed, do girls identify as much with Max as boys do?

MS: As many or more girls identify with Max. For one thing, he is wearing a unisex suit; you can't tell his gender. And any female child can look as maniacal as Max does. In the little plays that are put on by children all over the country, Max often is played by a little girl. In the opera, his role is sung by a soprano.

LSM: The backgrounds in the illustrations of *Wild Things* look like stage flats. They are not as fully rendered as the figures, who stand out contrastingly in relief, as do actors on a stage.

MS: I didn't think of that at the time, but it makes sense, if only because once the book was published, a ballet company in Boston choreographed *Wild Things* and an endless parade of musical people came along wanting to do something with it. The opera that eventually grew from it is wonderful and makes me happy.

LSM: Is *Outside Over There* (1981) still your favorite book, as you said it was at the time of its publication?

MS: *Higglety Pigglety Pop!* (1967) is my favorite in sentiment, because it is a tribute to my dog, Jennie, whom I loved so much, and because it is the only sad story I've ever written that turned out to be funny. But overall, *Outside Over There* is my favorite. I think it is the most beautifully structured book I've written. I never imagined that seven years later, I would still be doing a version of *Outside Over There*, but *Dear Mili* is an extension of that same

Maurice Sendak

subject—what can happen to vulnerable children. The two books belong together emotionally; *Dear Mili* is the grace note. It's the solution, the salvation.

LSM: The mother in *Outside Over There* looks really out of it as she sits in the arbor, waiting for her husband to return home from sea, and leaves it to her older daughter to take care of the baby. Do you think of the book as a fable for our times—as the story, with tragic overtones, of a withdrawn or irresponsible parent?

MS: No, I don't. The whole fantasy unfolds very quickly. It doesn't take twenty-four hours. You have a mother who for one moment thinks of something else: every mother does. And in that one moment something happens that she doesn't notice. I daresay it happens every single day. It's like Max and his mother. Now if Max's mother had been in a slightly better mood on that particular day, she wouldn't have screamed "Wild thing," and he wouldn't have said "I'll eat you up." She might have said what he really wanted her to say, which was, "Darling, you're hilarious, come and give Momma a hug," and he never would have gone on his journey, and there would have been no book. My books are all about that quirky minute when things just don't work out. Mothers were kids once, and they grow up to be just regular people. They cannot always be watching the child.

LSM: In *Outside Over There,* the sunflowers are watching out.

MS: Well, nature is watching out, and Ida is watching. She wishes to hell she didn't have a sister, and she wishes to hell that she wasn't dumped with this responsibility while Mother's sitting there gaga, and at that minute, she wishes this kid was dead and that she could be free. But the minute she wishes her dead, she unwishes it. That's what the book is about—this minute of distraction. And that's why I call those three books—*Wild Things, In the Night Kitchen* (1970), and *Outside Over There*—a trilogy. They're all about one minute's worth of distraction. One noise in the kitchen has Mickey doing a weird thing. One temper tantrum, one wrong word, causes all of the *Wild Things* to happen; one minute's dreamy distraction allows the kidnapping in *Outside Over There* to occur. I only have one subject. The one question I am obsessed with is, How do children survive?

LSM: When did you first think of the three books as a trilogy?

MS: When I did *Wild Things* I knew that it was such a good idea that I would have to play variations on it. Even then, I was thinking about it in musical terms. I wasn't going to make Max II; it had to be a different book about a wholly different world. And when *Night Kitchen* was done, it was full of exciting reverberations. Then it was on to the third variation. I somehow knew that the third book would have to be about a girl.

LSM: You have said that the baby in *Outside Over There* is Mili in your new book. I want to ask you about your personal mythology, how you come to make those connections.

MS: Well, it's all bits of things of my own particular life. Memories of things, social and political things that occurred in the world that frightened me as a child, things that I have to play with, re-create, or exorcise. The baby is immensely important because, as the youngest, I was the baby. I was always the baby, even when I got to be a middle-aged man. I grew up in the era of famous kidnapped babies, which played a part in *Outside Over There*. It was a re-creation of the Lindbergh kidnapping, which was so traumatic to me as a child. People say you mustn't frighten children, but you can't, because they already are frightened, they already know all these things. All you can do is console them.

LSM: Was this missing from your childhood experience?

MS: Nobody consoled me when Charles Lindbergh Jr. was found dead in the woods. It wasn't that my parents were cruel and therefore denied me consolation. It was that they wished I didn't know, and so they pretended to themselves that I didn't. For my part, I was too ashamed to ask, like the Henry James little girls who don't ask questions because they know it would be inappropriate. Well, I was a normal kid: I knew what was inappropriate—and I knew how to keep my mouth shut, even when I was dying to know.

So, like any normal kid, I made up my own answers. I thought, if a famous baby could die, a blond and beautiful baby, what could happen to an ugly, short, black-haired baby like me? *Outside Over There* was my fantasy in which the baby got saved. I changed history in that book. I did what I couldn't do: I brought him back alive. And I grew up to do a book that made it acceptable for me. Just as children take in everything and then, finally, because no one around them has the sense to explain the situation, they explain it to themselves. This is what my books are all about: explaining difficult life situations to myself.

LSM: *Dear Mili* is a Christian miracle tale. Was this story difficult for you, being Jewish, to illustrate?

MS: I saw it as a contemporary story of mothers forever gratuitously losing children because of the stupidity of men who go off soldiering. We read about it every day, in Vietnam, South Africa, you name it. In every country in the world, crying mothers and crying babies. It is the subject of human life. And for me, as a Jew, it was also very much the subject of the Holocaust: mothers and fathers separated from their children forever.

My father's entire family was destroyed in the Holocaust. I grew up in a house that was in a constant state of mourning. My Bar Mitzvah was one of the most tragic days in my father's life, which infuriated me; I didn't have the brains to understand what he was going through. That very morning a telegram arrived, saying that members of his family had been confirmed dead. I remember my father falling down, and me being in my little suit all ready to go, and the rage that was stirred in me by these dead Jews who constantly infiltrated our lives and made us miserable. But we got there, and they sang, "For He's a Jolly Good Fellow," and my brother and my mother held my father up on either side, and he got through it all. So it was very important for me to distill into this little story, however gently and subtly, my own Holocaust experience, to pay homage to those dead Jews. Their graves are in the book. Some of them are living in paradise with Mili and her guardian-angel friend.

LSM: Do you think some readers may find it strange to come upon these references in an overtly Christian story?

MS: I found it very appropriate to take this simple and very moving story and pay homage not just to Christian children but also to Jewish children, and black children, and Palestinian children, all of whom have died miserably and for no other reason than the stupidity of mankind.

LSM: In the illustrations of many of your books, you turn the gaze of the characters directly toward the reader. But in *Dear Mili*, the figures typically look away while the landscapes go wild all around them.

MS: The people in *Dear Mili* are symbolic. The mama of the story isn't Mrs. Jones down the street. The dramatic action did not so much lie in them. Then, where did it lie? I turned to the idea of a living forest. At the beginning, it's Arcadia. It's heaven for a minute. Then it's William Blake mad. Then it's early German Romantic glorioso. Then it's the sensuousness of English landscape painting. Then it's van Gogh going demented in paradise. This, of course, is an exaggerated, hyperbolic way of describing what I did. But I kept the book moving through nature.

LSM: At the beginning, when the war is mentioned, you have made the distant cannon fire look something like exploding sunflowers.

MS: I didn't think of that.

LSM: It calls to mind . . .

MS: *Outside Over There* . . . and Vincent van Gogh. It took steps to get to a religious story, a spiritual story. Van Gogh is one of the artists I trusted most to help me. He was a religious man and had wanted to be a priest when he was young. He had read the Bible and decided to go down into the coal mines and live with the poor. But the church fathers said, "Are you out of your mind? You're giving us a bad name!"—and kicked him out. And so he found another means to preach. He painted.

LSM: You seem to be describing van Gogh in much the same terms as you spoke earlier about children, as people who find their own answers to questions.

MS: Absolutely! I believe in sunflowers and in all the brazen, blazing pictures van Gogh painted and utterly trust his ecstatic vision.

LSM: Mark Twain once said that it's important never to let your schooling get in the way of your education. We've been talking just now about some of the artists from whose work you have learned. When you were young, however, you apparently did not enjoy going to school.

MS: But I have many honorary degrees! I wish to heaven my father was alive to see them, because I was the only child he could afford to send to college, and I was the only one of the three who refused to go. That was the irony of his life. If only he could have saved all that money by his son's just going off for a weekend and coming home with another degree. That would have made him so happy!

LSM: There's something very weighted and deliberate about the way you have drawn Mili; her feet are very big.

MS: I like to draw feet; one of the Wild Things has enormous feet. I have no interest, apparently, in proportion. But it does have another meaning when I draw children: these characters have a rootedness, they're planted.

I suppose what I love about Mili is that she's very much like the children in my other books. In spite of everything that's going on in her life, Mili proceeds with the kind of heroism that is natural to a normal child. She trusts her mother; when her mother says go, she goes, even though she doesn't comprehend why. And in a sense, she comes back as an emissary, as an angel, to take her mother to heaven with her. But she has the same kind of trudging, hardworking quality that I love in children. They're trudging children; they go and do what they must do.

INTERVIEW 2: JULY 14, 1993

LEONARD S. MARCUS: Your new book, *We Are All in the Dumps with Jack and Guy*, has the intensity of a fever dream. It must have grown out of some compelling inner need. What was that need?

MAURICE SENDAK: Partly, it was an old artistic conundrum. I actually began *Dumps* in the mid-1960s, right after *Hector Protector* (1965). I was so entranced with nursery rhymes then that I wanted to do another book right afterward that, from my point of view, would be more accomplished than the first one. The two rhymes in *Hector* aren't joined in any way except by the slim fact that both are about rather repellent little boys. I wanted something more complicated than that for the second book.

I had done a lot of research in the nursery rhymes, found "Dumps" and "Jack," and did a dummy for the new book. I didn't like the dummy, and so I put it away. But I kept it, because I knew that a rhyme called "We Are All in the Dumps" was made for me!

That was part of the urgency, as it continued to cook in my little Night Kitchen brain for all these thirty-odd years. Then, one night, when I was in Los Angeles to work on an opera, I was driving down a very posh street on the way back to my hotel and saw a kid sleeping in a box. His naked feet were sticking out of the box. The juxtaposition of the posh street and the kid just seemed crazy, and it made me think of the two nursery rhymes that I had come across so many years earlier. A little later, I did some research and found that Rio de Janeiro is circled by shantytowns with just children living in them, and that those children have created their own little society, which is what happens in my book. Anyway, the idea started to come to life, and it just hooked into the old rhymes, which now suddenly had a whole new meaning.

With *Dumps* there was also the excitement for me of doing a book that was not quite about me. Suddenly, I felt free to do such a book in which my self was not the central subject.

LSM: Does that freedom come with age?

MS: I think it comes with age. It also confirms what I said many years ago, but that only now makes sense to me, that *Outside Over There* would be my last picture book. What I meant, really, was that it was the last picture book that was to be an excavation of my soul, the last archaeological Sendakian dig! I think I only knew it was the last when, later, I was doing the illustrations for *I Saw Esau* (1992) and found myself thinking, My God, I'm happy doing this book. That must mean I'm free.

LSM: You could be describing an end to therapy.

MS: In a sense, yes—a very rich sense. Critics have said that the book was a throwback, an attempt to recapture my earlier styles of illustration. I wasn't conscious of anything of the kind. I just knew that the verses were jubilant and that I was working on a book without the familiar anxieties and inhibitions that had been part of my entire creative life—a very functional part to be sure—until then.

It was like shedding a snakeskin, and *Dumps* is definitely the child of *Esau*.

LSM: The illustrations in *Dumps* could be camera close-ups of the tableaux you drew for *I Saw Esau*.

MS: Precisely. With more than a decade's career on the operatic stage behind me, there is also a theatricality about the book that I'm very proud of.

LSM: Both rhymes are cryptic. Was Iona Opie able to give you any special insight into their meaning?

MS: She said nothing was known about them. I made some minor changes. The original of one line reads: "The babies are bit." I changed that to: "The baby is bit." So I asked Iona, "Is this kosher?" She laughed and said, "That's what they're for!" That is exactly what they are for: to transform and change and use over and over again.

LSM: The headlines that appear on the cover and elsewhere throughout the illustrations are very contemporary.

MS: The device of the newspaper headlines developed as I composed the book. It came, as often happens, as the solution to practical problems. For instance, when the moon cries, you have a choice. Do the kids have umbrellas to keep themselves from getting soaked? Well, if they don't have houses, they don't have umbrellas. So what do they use? Newspapers, old newspapers. So the newspapers became their clothing, and they became their "houses without walls." I then thought, the newspapers must say something, but what? Once you are putting in headlines, why not headlines that have a satiric edge, even a painful edge?

LSM: Some are very painful. Do you think that news about homelessness and AIDS are having the same kind of impact on children now as the Lindbergh kidnapping did on you as a child?

M S : Of course. It seems to me that there are so many more ferocious horrors—stories of children getting shot on the way to school; the story of a four-year-old leaving his sibling to die at a fire; and hospitals jammed with AIDS babies. They make me and my Lindbergh fantasy seem small stuff.

L S M : Hasn't most of children's literature been based on the premise that kids can somehow be protected from the harsher realities?

M S : Yes, but that runs counter to what I firmly believe, which is that children *do* know what's going on. I mean, when the Lindbergh baby was kidnapped, I knew at age four that something had happened to this child that could happen to me. I think that all small children know things we wish they didn't. But wishing is not going to make that go away. Of course, you don't want to tell kids about things that are beyond their comprehension or that are unlikely to happen. The idea that children today know that they can be shot on the way to school petrifies my brain, because I don't know what they do with that knowledge.

L S M : So there's no way kids can escape from an awareness of that kind of violence and suffering?

M S : There's just no protecting them. We're confronted with a terrible dilemma, which is having to tell children things that we know are hard for them to hear, yet that they have to know to protect their lives. It's like not wanting to put the word *condom* into a sex-education pamphlet. Kids have sex so much earlier now, but people don't want to use the word *condom*. I mean, if you want to kill kids, why don't you take them out in the street and shoot them? Why not help them instead? When do we give up this nonsense about words that are not permissible and knowledge that is not permissible, if in fact they save lives? It's a phony morality.

L S M : In its depiction of homelessness and references to AIDS, your book makes an angry appeal for an end to the moral complacency of our society. Shouldn't that kind of plea be addressed to adults, not children?

MS: Absolutely—in fact, this book is also being marketed to adults. I didn't fight for that, but it was a blessing that it turned out that way. I've been struggling with the constraints of being a children's book illustrator/writer for years. The discomfort has nothing to do with my passion for children, but with grown-ups there's always the subtle implication that your work is not very important. That's always plagued us in this business. The book does take up some serious issues with adults, such as where the hell are they in an emergency?

LSM: But what about the child reader?

MS: What the book really says is, You kids are heroes. You'll make out. Children will persevere if they can. They'll find a family. That's all they need, that's all they want—to be loved and cared for and fed. That's what I hope children will see in it.

What sort of message do children get out of *Hansel and Gretel*, one of the most dire tales ever written? That story is like a punch in the face. Do they get any joy out of hearing that the stepmother loathes them and wishes them dead? That the father is a wimp? It's only their own courage and resilience that keep Hansel and Gretel alive. Now, *Dumps* is no more frightening than that famous story.

LSM: But *Hansel and Gretel*, like other fairy tales, takes place in a vague, once-upon-a-time fantasy realm, while your story has the immediacy of the morning's headlines. Doesn't that make your story scarier?

MS: It may to you, and to other grown-ups, but not to the kids hearing it. All that once-upon-a-time stuff is cosmetic embroidery, a device. Who has time for devices these days? Adults don't and children don't. I think the world is in a dire situation, and I'm surely not alone in feeling that is so. So why hold it off at a distance? It doesn't make sense to do that anymore.

LSM: The word "AIDS" recurs, like a mantra, in the newspapers of your illustrations.

MS: My life has been totally changed by the loss of my friends, so many I can't count. How do we not talk about it? It's like trying to keep your mouth shut about something that is devouring you. But the big question will be, Is this appropriate for children?

LSM: What is your answer?

MS: There will be people who will object to AIDS as a subtext of this tale. I couldn't care less. If people condemn me, fine. If they are tired of the subject and angry at this book, fine. If they want to put their heads in the sand, fine. Don't tell me children don't know about AIDS. That's ridiculous!

LSM: Do you feel that by creating this book you have become a political activist?

MS: Yes, but I don't want *Dumps* to be seen as a political tract. It's still me, it's still a picture book to be read and, I hope, enjoyed. It still has all my idiosyncratic fantasies, and to me it is no different from the subject of any other book I've ever done: It is about the heroism of children. Kids see that. You know, things get simplified so fast. This book is not suddenly stripping away everything I've ever done and making me a political commentator. No way.

LSM: But for you, dealing with a subject like AIDS is something new.

MS: When you lose good friends who are much younger than you, then you begin to see the world as upside down. Students I adored, whose work was magnificent, who were far more gifted than I was at their age, are dead and gone. Older people whose work I admired are gone. It takes my breath away. It's become a part of my life, part of my nervous system, part of my terrible grief. If that makes me political, so be it. There is grief in this book, but there is also joy. I know there is because I felt joy doing it.

WAYS OF TELLING

LSM: You are old enough now to be a grandparent. Often grandparents have a different, more relaxed relationship with children than do parents. Has there been a comparable change in your relationship to your audience, or in the way you make books for children?

MS: That is a curious and interesting thought. It must be true to some extent, because when you are young, you are caught up in the intensity of recovery, of truth-telling, of making sure you got it right.

LSM: Recovery from what?

MS: From your own childhood. So, yes, I would say the grandfather metaphor is suitable.

LSM: Notwithstanding the book's intensity, there's a very relaxed feeling to the drawing style of *Dumps*.

MS: You see I'm no longer concerned with drawing. I'm counting on many decades of experience to come through for me; style and technique have become second nature. My heroes, too, have become a part of me in my old age: Dickens, Blake, everybody I've ripped off and stolen from! Instead of paying homage to them as a trembling student, as I did in my earlier works, I feel as if I've swallowed them whole.

One of the few graces of getting old—and God knows there are few graces—is that if you've worked hard and kept your nose to the grindstone, something happens: the body gets old, but the creative mechanism is refreshed, smoothed and oiled and honed. That is the grace. That is the splendid grace. And I think that is what's happening to me. I'm afraid of getting old. I'm afraid of my body failing me. And yet there's this other side, this young side. Mama mia! How many people can claim such a thing?

················

William Steig

Born November 14, 1907
Brooklyn, New York

with

Jeanne Steig

Born May 2, 1930
Chicago, Illinois

....

W illiam Steig had long been one of The
New Yorker *magazine's most illustri-
ous artists when, at a friend's prompting, he first
turned his attention to picture book making. He
was nearly sixty years old at the time. His first
two children's books,* Roland the Minstrel Pig
and C D B!, *both appeared in 1968. Steig was
honored for his third picture book,* Sylvester
and the Magic Pebble *(1969), with the
Caldecott Medal for 1970.*

*Although known primarily as a visual artist, Steig is also an inspired
writer whose stories for young readers combine the dreamlike strangeness
and precision of fairy tales with the teasing wit of the artist's own cartoons.
Powerful emotions color and shape even the most comically far-fetched
situations, as when in* Doctor De Soto *(1982) a sympathetic dentist
mouse risks death to treat a surly fox in pain.*

Steig is at once a very funny and a very serious man. Chatting over a brown-bag lunch, he is quick to investigate the comic potential in the sour pickle placed before him and the sculptural possibilities of a nearby pair of plastic forks. As his story about the magic pebble would seem to confirm, nothing in this artist's world is too small or insignificant to merit its fair share of attention.

Steig met and married his fourth wife, Jeanne, a sculptor and writer, in the mid-sixties. Among the children's books they have collaborated on are Consider the Lemming (1988), A Handful of Beans (1998), and A Gift from Zeus (2001).

We recorded this interview in the Steigs' spacious, art-filled Boston apartment on July 14, 1994.

WILLIAM STEIG: Interviewers always ask me the same questions, like, How'd you get into this racket? Stuff like that.

LEONARD S. MARCUS: I promise not to ask you that.

WS: You can. . . .

LSM: I would like to ask you about your new book, *Zeke Pippin* (1994). It feels as if you were revisiting some of your earlier books in this more recent one.

WS: I do that all the time. Apparently, I've written only one book and keep varying it.

LSM: For instance, in *Farmer Palmer's Wagon Ride* (1974) there's a pig named Zeke who gets a harmonica from his father as a present.

JEANNE STEIG: I didn't remember that pig's name was Zeke.

WS: I didn't either! It certainly wasn't conscious. Ezekiel, by the way, is my favorite name. If I had another son I'd call him Zeke.

LSM: You like the way the name sounds?

WS: What else is there to like?

LSM: There's the biblical association.

WS: Oh, that association doesn't mean anything to me.

LSM: Did you ever want to be a musician?

WS: No, but my son is a great musician, a jazz flutist.

LSM: The reason I ask is that music plays a part in so many of your stories.

WS: I think that's because of my son, and because I had a brother who played jazz music.

LSM: Music sometimes even saves the life of the heroes of your stories; for instance, in *Roland the Minstrel Pig*. If Roland hadn't been playing his lute when the king came along, he would have fried.

JS: The bone in *The Amazing Bone* (1976) does a sort of trumpet number when it's trying to save Pearl.

LSM: And Farmer Palmer is able to stop the runaway wheel in its tracks by playing on the very harmonica that he is bringing home for his son. So music takes on the power of magic.

WS: And Farmer Palmer is a pig, right? Pigs would be the last animals who'd play harmonicas because they can't purse their lips the way you're supposed to. It worried me that in the book he doesn't really look like he's playing.

LSM: You've said elsewhere that *Pinocchio* is a book that meant a lot to you as a child.

WS: I loved it as a kid. Still love it. In fact, I read it every few years. I know Sendak finds fault with it. He likes Disney's *Pinocchio* better, which seems insane to me. There's something about the moralizing of the original *Pinocchio* that bothers him. He's right about that— but it's still a good story!

LSM: At various points in the story, both Pinocchio and Gepetto stand falsely accused of various misdeeds, and in the end Pinocchio has to find his way back to his father in order to make amends. That element of the story resembles, does it not, the plot of *The Real Thief* (1973), which is also about the burden of living with false accusations?

WS: In that connection, I remember that any time a teacher of mine said, "Who stole so-and-so's fountain pen?" I always felt guilty.

LSM: You mean even if you hadn't actually done it?

WS: Never did anything, no. But somehow I always felt they were gonna accuse me.

JS: Bill had three brothers, and it was always important to all four of them to establish "who did it."

WS: Who was responsible for some misdeed.

LSM: So you were afraid of being accused?

WS: I just felt guilty, like "I almost did it," or "I could have done it." I don't know.

JS: You feel guilty if you see a cop!

WS: I feel guilty if I'm driving and I see a cop.

JS: When you're driving, you usually are!

LSM: Another possible connection between *Pinocchio* and your stories is that Pinocchio starts out as a piece of scrap wood.

WS: You mean, the harmonica's garbage, too?

JS: You have a whole book about a garbage collector, *Tiffky Doofky* (1978). And [to WS] you married a garbage collector. I collect junk. [to LSM] . . . and make sculpture out of it. I'm a sculptor.

WS: When we walk down the streets of New York, I've got to keep her away from garbage cans.

LSM: Does the idea of "found objects" appeal to you aesthetically?

WS: No.

JS: What about that storage battery you found when you were a child?

WS: Oh, right. When I was two years old, we moved from Brooklyn to the Bronx, and I found in the garbage can outside our house—kids could hang out in the street in those days without getting killed—I found a storage battery, one of those things shaped like a tall glass, and it was beautiful, everything was clean, sharp. And I said, "Look at the beautiful things people throw away."

LSM: Is that your earliest childhood memory?

WS: No. I can remember my first automobile ride. This was before I was two. Somebody let me sit next to him in his automobile. This new miracle. That was in Brooklyn.

LSM: Were you thrilled by the ride?

WS: I remember being impressed that this thing was moving without horses. Most vehicles were horse-drawn when I was young. I also remember that, when I was very young, a certain kid came into our house and I wanted him kicked out, but my mother told him he could stay. That got me really angry. I remember that as an injustice.

LSM: You wanted all the attention for yourself?

WS: No. Something this kid did displeased me, and I told him, "Get out!" But she said, "You can't do that." So I felt she had betrayed me by letting him stay.

LSM: Going back to found objects, Sylvester finds something—not junk, but an ordinary pebble—that turns out to have magical properties.

WS: I guess it might be related to my searching in garbage cans. But Sylvester didn't find the pebble in a garbage can, did he?

LSM: My idea was just that the pebble is such an ordinary thing that most people wouldn't have thought it worth keeping.

WS: Are you trying to say something about my psychology?

LSM: Not in so many words. [laughter]

JS: Good luck to you!

LSM: I'm just trying to see what your stories have in common with each other.

WS: You mean what motivates me? You know, I've said in interviews that I do it for money. Why do you write stories? That's the way I make my living. One doesn't always analyze why one does something. I began writing kids' stories because Robert Kraus said he was going to be a publisher. He said, "Will you write a story for me?" I said, "Sure." And it's what enabled me to give up drawing for advertising, which I always felt unclean about, because I didn't think that was a proper function for art, to sell things, except to sell itself.

LSM: Did you find that you enjoyed writing?

WS: I'd often thought of writing when I was young, you know, like every other guy. In fact, I occasionally wrote a few pages and thought it sounded pretty good. I never thought of selling my writing except when I was young. I thought it might be a nice way to make a living. I'm probably one of the few guys that enjoys what he does. Somebody told me that it must be less than one percent of the population that enjoys what they do.

LSM: I wouldn't be surprised.

WS: I wouldn't be surprised either. And even I'm not satisfied, because I do some things just because they're practical, like write another story. But once I get into it I enjoy it.

LSM: Did you draw much as a child?

WS: Not really. We were encouraged by my old man to copy things. He thought that was a good way to learn to draw, by copying things.

LSM: Do you think that's true?

WS: I don't know if it's true or untrue. The best way to start somebody drawing is to give him or her a pencil and paper.

LSM: Your father was an amateur artist himself, wasn't he?

WS: Yeah. There's something on one of these walls that he did. He encouraged me to draw, but mostly he encouraged me to make some money because he felt he had supported me for long enough. This was when I was fifteen and was starting college. I worked for him in the summertime. He was a house painter, and he used to pay me in malteds. At the end of the day, he'd buy me a malted. He figured I owed him these days of work because he'd worked for me up until then. Anyway, he supported me for something like twenty years, and then I supported him for twenty-five years in greater style than he supported me. But he was a nice guy. I make him sound like he was some kind of a bad egg.

LSM: Did your mother also paint?

WS: Yes. She was very good. That's hers over there [pointing toward the living room]. See the cow? To the right of the cow there's a [painting of a] vase with daisies in it. Everything in this house was done by a friend or a relative.

LSM: If your father wanted you to make money, he made an unusual choice when he urged you to become an artist.

WS: Here's something I say very often. My father was a Socialist, and he couldn't afford to send us to school to become professionals. He said, "If you work for someone you're being exploited. If you're the boss you're the exploiter." He said both of those are undesirable positions to be in. So he encouraged the arts.

LSM: Were there a lot of like-minded people living in your neighborhood?

WS: He had a lot of European friends, and they were all Socialists.

LSM: You did go to art school . . .

WS: Yes. First, I got into City College when I was still fifteen. I spent most of my time there in the swimming pool and, in fact, was on the swimming team. My father didn't think my life at the school was preparing me for the future. Then somehow I got into art school, something called the National Academy of Design Art School. My father was pushing me. Then briefly I was in the Yale School of Fine Arts, but I was disappointed in the school. So in the middle of the night one night I packed my bag, and I sneaked out of the house of the friend I was staying with in New Haven and came home.

LSM: Were you interested in the experimental art movements of the time, for example in surrealism?

ws: No. In those days there were very few people who were influenced by modern art. Stuart Davis was influenced by the Armory Show in 1913. But, no, I didn't appreciate modern art when I was in my late teens or twenties. I didn't appreciate van Gogh or Cézanne either, though my kid brother did.

lsm: Was there a point at which that changed for you?

ws: Of course. Otherwise, I would have remained a dodo.

lsm: You did those books of symbolic drawings during the 1930s and 1940s.

ws: You're going to ask me, How come?

lsm: Certainly not!

ws: All that stuff embarrasses me.

lsm: In the foreword to one of those books, *About People*, there's a reference to various theories of automatic drawing. Is that an idea or technique that has been especially important to you?

ws: That's the way I start drawing sometimes. I draw without knowing what I want to do. Sometimes interesting things happen.

lsm: Do you think of it as a kind of daydreaming?

ws: I don't think of it that way, no. It's something that happens after I've been drawing for a while, and it only happens when I'm alone. There are a lot of *New Yorker* artists who work right in the office. You can stop by, chew the fat with them, and they just keep on working on their drawings. I can't understand that. In fact, even here in my own house I can't draw if somebody's visiting Jeanne three rooms away. And I noticed living in the country that I always did my very best work when I was snowed in.

lsm: Are you often surprised by what you draw?

ws: Not oversurprised, but things happen that you don't expect. But you're not interested in my drawing.

lsm: Sure I am.

ws: If I change my paper and my pen, a whole lot of things happen, because sometimes . . . I've found a rough paper will steer you in a different direction, make you think along different lines—the fact that your hand is doing this [rather than that] brings something else out. When I'm illustrating my kids' books, as compared to when I'm just drawing, I feel very constrained because I like to draw on impulse, not because "now he's standing under a tree . . ."

LSM: You spoke before about a childhood experience that left you feeling betrayed by your mother. Similar feelings would seem to be in the background of *Zeke Pippin.*

WS: All kids feel misunderstood. Did you feel misunderstood as a kid? Of course kids are misunderstood. How can you understand a kid unless you are one?

LSM: So you weren't drawing on a particular memory when you wrote that story?

WS: No, never consciously. What would suggest that?

LSM: Just that, as in other stories of yours, the emotion is so strongly felt that it doesn't seem it could have been contrived.

WS: That's a compliment!

LSM: I think so.

WS: You mean the writing sounds like it was felt? I'm not aware that the story is related to any experience. I'd have to look at the book again.

LSM: *Spinky Sulks* (1988) is another story about a kid who feels burned by his family's treatment of him.

WS: I don't think that's from my experience. I mean not directly. I couldn't sulk when I was a kid. My father would give me a kick in the ass if I sulked too much.

LSM: The story could be wish fulfillment, then. [laughter] Your drawings of Spinky, Irene, and Leonard remind me a little of Crockett Johnson's drawings of kids.

WS: I wasn't a big admirer of his.

LSM: Your child characters, though, like his, look very solid. Do you think of children as being durable, able to take care of themselves?

WS: No, I don't. I think kids are very fragile actually, sensitive, easily hurt. Don't you? I guess they have both qualities—sensitivity and strength.

LSM: Irene goes out into the storm and is battered by the elements, but somehow manages to get through it all.

WS: Yeah, but I don't think that's related to my experiences. I mean everybody's been out in the snow and . . . as an adult I had trouble once in a snowstorm getting home because I was on foot and the snow was falling very fast . . .

LSM: There really are so many storms in your books.

WS: I love storms. I just love them.

LSM: Do you seek them out?

WS: Not now, but I remember when I started living in the country, I used to love to run out in a big thunderstorm to get wet, start screaming with the thunder, stuff like that. Storms are dramatic. Everybody likes that. There's also something nice about being sheltered indoors when it's stormy outside, and looking out, and feeling you're secure, and that you'd rather be in than out.

LSM: As a city child, did you already have a strong feeling for nature?

WS: I think it's automatic that kids love nature. I can remember in the Bronx, the first time I saw a tomato growing in a lot—a junk lot. Somebody apparently had dropped a tomato there, obviously it was in the garbage. And here was this tomato hanging out on the plant. It was like a revelation to me. When I was a kid there was a lot of natural world around. There were parks; we saw trees.

When I lived on Brook Avenue in the Bronx, the New York Central Railroad ran past our house. We were on Brook, then there was the railroad, and then there was Park Avenue. And choo-choo trains would come right past our window, with big smoke and all that. And then there were bridges going from Brook Avenue to Park Avenue, across this depression where the trains ran. And when the train came by there'd be a lot of smoke and steam. So that when the kids saw one coming they'd get up on these bridges to get enveloped in this smoke and steam. It was part of our fun. "Hey, the train's coming!"

LSM: I would like to ask you about your work for *The New Yorker*. Did the artists who worked for the magazine get to know each other?

WS: Yeah, sure. I started during the Depression. *The New Yorker* paid forty dollars a drawing in those days. The next payer was something like fifteen dollars. There were two magazines called *Life* and *Judge* that also printed humorous drawings. So you'd always go to *The New Yorker* first, then you'd go to *Life* and *Judge*. And the last place you'd send a drawing to was the five-dollar market. During the Depression there were a lot of little magazines that printed cartoons—humor—which they thought the people needed because of the Depression.

Now here's a story I tell everybody about *The New Yorker*. I submitted my first cover, and they said, "We like the idea but not your rendition." You know, we don't think it's good enough. "Can we buy the idea from you?" So I said, "Let me think it over." I came home and told my mother, and she said, "Don't do that! Don't sell them the idea. They'll always expect you to sell 'em the idea." So when I came back the next day I said, "My mother told me not to sell you the idea." So they said, "Okay, we'll take the cover as it is." That was my first cover. I'd been working for them a while by then. Anyway, that's one of my stories.

LSM: Were the drawings in your books first published in *The New Yorker*?

WS: No, no. There was a book called *The Lonely Ones* (1942). The

New Yorker turned that down, and Ross regretted it afterward because it proved to be very popular.

LSM: You must have gotten to know E. B. White.

WS: E. B. White invited me to a gathering at his house when I first worked for *The New Yorker*. I sat around; I was too scared to say a word, and he never asked me again. I guess he felt I wasn't comfortable. I was a shy, shy kid.

LSM: Maybe he was shy, too.

WS: Not from my perspective. He wasn't shy at that gathering.

LSM: Did you become interested in his children's books at some point?

WS: Not especially, no. I saw them, sure. I always admired them.

LSM: You and he write about the beauty of the universe in much the same terms.

WS: That's a natural thing to do. The universe is beautiful.

LSM: Have you read William Blake? I feel there is a lot of Blake's "The Tyger" in your children's books.

WS: Oh, yeah? He's one of my favorite writers.

LSM: For instance, in *Amos & Boris* (1971), it's just when Amos the mouse is floating along, admiring the beauty of everything, that he rolls off the deck of his boat and is sent scrambling for his life into the water.

WS: And you relate that to Blake? That's amazing. I love Blake. I used to . . . Every time I saw a book with Blake things I would buy it. I don't understand a lot of what he writes, but I know it's wonderful. He's one of my heroes. Was. Because I don't think about him now.

LSM: Were you interested in his visual art, his illustrations?

WS: No, I couldn't get into that. I don't think of myself as that good an artist. My work has become good, in an unusual way. And I know I have influenced a lot of people. A lot of people who draw children, for instance, say they learned how to draw kids from me, from look-ing at my stuff. I was able to draw certain expressions that hadn't been done before.

LSM: When you did the drawing for *The Lonely Ones* that bears the caption "People are no damn good," did you mean it to refer only to adults or to children also?

WS: Only adults, of course. It's interesting about that book. I got a letter from a chaplain who said that the book had had a very sooth-ing effect on guys who had been through the Battle of Iwo Jima. I used to cherish that letter. Soldiers aren't necessarily the most cul-tivated guys. Usually not. But somehow this book affected them.

LSM: Did you know A. S. Neill, the founder of the experimental English boarding school Summerhill?

WS: Oh, you know that I was associated with Wilhelm Reich, then, who was Neill's teacher. No, I never met Neill. But, of course, I met Reich.

LSM: You said somewhere that you consider Reich one of the most important people of our time.

WS: I think he was the most important person of this century.

LSM: What was the essence of his greatness?

WS: He demonstrated that space is not empty but filled with what he called orgone energy. He discovered, for example, that a stone, though not alive, is full of energy, which is alive. That when you die, your matter dies but not your energy. That people's great prob-lem is that their energy is bound up in what he called muscular armature; in other words, that most people are standing on their own balls most of the time.

LSM: Did you think of some of your early drawings as depictions of people who were "armored" in the Reichian sense?

WS: Yeah, that's true—of *The Lonely Ones*, for example. When I met Reich, he had that book on his table. He liked it. Then later I illustrated a book of his. He was a remarkable man. He could look at you and tell you all about yourself. For example, when I was in treatment with him once, I came in and lay down on the couch, and then he came in and said, "Oh! I see you're a clown today." There was nothing clownish about me. But all morning before seeing him I had been doodling and drawing clowns. I would have said that was just arbitrary. It could have been devils, could have been something else. But he saw something. Then I realized that when I draw a clown, it's not just an arbitrary choice.

LSM: A. S. Neill wrote about the "self-regulating child."

WS: That was a phrase of Reich's, too. I guess he meant that children naturally have a lot to do with their own well-being. That doesn't mean they don't need help. They're still children. But they start out life having sound natural impulses relating to their basic needs.

LSM: Reichian therapy then was a stripping away of the "armor" to get back to those sound impulses?

WS: Yes, it worked best when he was the therapist. Also, the effect isn't necessarily permanent because the guy goes right back into the same society that fucked him up to start with.

LSM: I have a theory you're probably not going to like. It concerns Reich and your book *Shrek!* (1990). Reich apparently thought there were three layers to people. There was the armored outer layer. Then there was a second layer where your wild, aggressive impulses come out. . . .

WS: The outer level is the artificial person—what you present to society. In between is the dreck. And underneath that is the beautiful human being.

LSM: Well, here's my idea: could the "dreck" be Shrek? He's an ogre at first, and it's only after he comes to the room where he has to face himself in all the mirrors that he becomes capable of falling in love.

ws: I guess there is some of that in there. Sure. Reich wound up in jail and died of a heart attack. They burned his books. Did you know that? His work is still available, but no one has latched on to it. But when I first read a book by Reich, I said I always knew that some-body had the answer to what our problems are, and I thought, this is it. So I went right to him.

································

Rosemary Wells

Born January 29, 1943
New York, New York

....

osemary Wells first hit her stride as a picture book artist in the early 1970s with
stories for preschoolers that gave both young
and old something to smile about, while pulling
no punches about the emotional bumps and
bruises all children endure. Wells rendered
Benjamin and Tulip (1973), Noisy Nora
(1973; 1997), and other picture books from
this time with the admirable economy of a film
short or vaudeville sketch. But by the late
1970s, she had distilled her approach still further. With the publication in
1979 of her first set of board books about Max and Ruby, Wells set the
standard for a genre then in its infancy. In those landmark books, she
demonstrated the possibility, within the space of a few small pages, of lay-
ing down memorable characters in fully developed stories laced with
strong emotional crosscurrents and a robust sense of fun.

Although trained as a visual artist, Wells has always felt more at home
with words. In addition to the many picture books she has both written
and illustrated, she has also authored fiction for older readers, including
Through the Hidden Door (1987) and Mary on Horseback (1998).
In recent years, in part out of concern for the literacy level of children
in the television age, Wells has reillustrated or recast a wide variety of

children's classics, from Mother Goose *rhymes to* Lassie Come-Home *(1995), with a view to helping to ensure their continued survival.*

We recorded this interview in New York City on October 18, 1999.

LEONARD S. MARCUS: What kind of child were you?

ROSEMARY WELLS: Very cheerful. Very focused and directed. Very stubborn. I would do anything I liked with a passion and was completely unwilling to do anything I didn't see any reason to do—math, for instance. So, as you can imagine, I did not do very well in school.

LSM: When did you become interested in art?

RW: I was drawing, apparently, at the age of two and a half. My mother was my first editor. She had a system. Every Friday evening, for as long as I can remember, she would take all my drawings for the week and pick the good ones that, as she put it, were to "go up." This meant that the drawings she had chosen would be thumbtacked to the mantelpiece and kept on display until the following Friday. My mother would say, "These are wonderful"—and just ignore the rest. That is how I learned what was good.

I was so supported and loved by both my parents. My father was a writer and my mother was a dancer, and I think they both must have said, "Ah, well this is wonderful. Of course she's an artist, and this is what she'll do." They were very glad that I wasn't a dancer because my mother hadn't liked parts of that life very much—all the travel and the physical ordeal. But they welcomed the life of an artist. Money was never discussed in my family. The point was to do a thing well and then money would come.

LSM: You were an only child. Yet you have written and illustrated so many books about sibling rivalry. Has doing those books been a way for you to imagine a childhood you feel you missed?

RW: No, I wouldn't say so. For one thing, I was only sort of an only child in that I had a half brother, Peter, whom I saw on weekends and in the summertime. I cannot really say why I do lots of books about sibling rivalries. Since I've had children, obviously, it's partly because I have two children. But I did *Morris's Disappearing Bag* (1975; 1999) long before I had children. It had to do with an outside awareness that I can't explain, and not much to do with exploring my own experiences.

LSM: I think that *Morris's Disappearing Bag* is quite a strange book. The image of the magic bag has a seemingly mythic dimension.

RW: Well, there are three great dreams of childhood. One is to have eyes in the back of your head. One is to fly. And the third dream is to be able to disappear. I remember very clearly as a child seeing on television Jean Cocteau's *Orpheus*, about a man who could walk through walls. I was fascinated with that idea. I could not believe how wonderful it was. He even got out of jail by walking through the cell wall. So I was always interested in oddities of that kind. I think that is because I was brought up by a mother who, although she was born in New York City and was an American, had a Russian soul and learned all sorts of superstitions from her fellow dancers in the *Ballets Russes de Monte Carlo*. She believed in all sorts of strange things. I was close enough to it all as a child to take this kind of belief completely for granted: even if I did not believe it myself, I accepted that it was part of the world.

LSM: Tell me more about your parents.

RW: My father, whose name was James Warwick, was a playwright. His drama, *Blind Alley*, was produced on the *Playhouse 90* television series and later made into a rather well-known film called *The Desperate Hours*. My father came close to being blacklisted during the McCarthy era because his best friend was Melvyn Douglas and Melvyn's wife, Helen Gahagan Douglas, ran against Richard Nixon

Rosemary Wells

for Congress and was smeared horribly during her unsuccessful campaign. My father stood up for Helen and became so closely associated with the Douglases that the McCarthy people started looking at him. He stopped writing after that episode and never wrote again. He was a wonderful writer.

From the time I was tiny my parents made me so aware of language and its power, its poetry and music. We had classical music playing in the house all the time. They believed that culture should enlighten people, not pander to them.

The one single experience I can remember from my childhood that is so relevant to what I do and to how I feel about my work is just a very slight memory without words. It's a memory of my mother when I was very, very tiny, probably three, stacking the Victrola with 78 records of *Giselle* or *Coppélia* and . . . I can see her! She has on her sailor shorts with three little buttons on each side and a halter. It's summertime. . . . And she put on that music, and she simply danced all through the house. She did the whole ballet. From that experience I learned just how it is with art. No one said to her, "Now do this." She simply danced to that music and became the dance. It just came to her out of the air. It came from heaven.

LSM: Compared to all this, school must have seemed a little boring.

RW: For the most part, yes. But I had lots of friends and fun, too.

LSM: What kinds of books did you read as a child?

RW: I read absolutely everything. Not nearly as many children's books were published in the 1940s and 1950s as are published now. But so many of the books of that time were very well written and had a comforting factor to them for children, as if the author was saying, "Hey, I'm really on your side, and I understand who you are and no one else does!" I didn't mind reading the same books over and over again. I used to pile up all my favorite books in bed when I wasn't feeling well, and I would read them all morning long if I stayed home from school or if it was a rainy day. Then I'd listen on the radio to my favorite melodrama, *The Romance of Helen Trent*— "Can a girl from a little mining town in the West find happiness as the wife of a wealthy and titled Englishman?" I loved it! Then I would go back to my reading in the afternoon.

I loved the Beatrix Potter series. I loved everything that Robert Lawson wrote and illustrated. His books were magic to me, particularly the longer ones such as *The Great Wheel* and *Mr. Revere and I*. Those books made me love history, which was also my father's great passion. History was one subject I always did well in at school.

LSM: Did the art you saw in books become connected in your mind with the art you yourself were making as a child?

RW: Oh, yes. Everything I saw in books I copied. But I wasn't just looking at children's books. My grandmother had an enormous house with a huge library in which I saw, for instance, *The New Yorker* cartoon books and books by the English political cartoonist David Lowe.

LSM: What about comic books, which many parents of that era tried to discourage their children from reading? Did your parents feel differently?

RW: My mother hated comic books and forbade them. But I got hold of them anyway. I just learned to keep them away from her.

LSM: What prompted you to become an artist who made books and, in particular, children's books?

RW: I didn't have any idea that I was going to become a children's book artist, not even in art school at the Museum School in Boston, which was a hotbed of Abstract Expressionism. What happened was that I got married, and then I needed a job. We needed money. My first job was as an assistant buyer in purses and bags for the Lorraine shops in Boston. That lasted about a week. My second job was as a salesgirl at Lauriat's bookstore. That was close but no cigar. I still didn't know what to do. I knew I could draw, however, and I thought, There must be a way you can get a life as an artist. How do you do it? I decided to try the Boston publishing companies, knowing that they published illustration. My portfolio consisted of invented book jackets for all my favorite classics. They were terrible but wild. I brought them around to Allyn and Bacon, where I was hired to substitute for an art department file clerk who had gone away for the summer. I completely ignored the files and threw myself into an American history book with a passion. By the time the summer was over, I was already editing and was given a permanent position as a book designer. I never had to worry again. Over the next six years I parlayed that first work experience into other jobs, learning the business as I went along, and then became an illustrator, and then also a writer.

After we moved to New York, where my husband was studying architecture at Columbia, I got a job at Macmillan. Susan Hirschman headed the children's book department, and one day I gave Susan a little dummy I had done of a Gilbert and Sullivan song. She accepted it on the spot and published it. She said to me, "Sit down, Rosemary. You're a Macmillan author now!" Except perhaps for "Marry me!" those were the most wonderful words I ever heard. I did sit down, and Susan proceeded to show me dozens of books from Harper, where she had worked under Ursula Nordstrom. She spent hours teaching me what was appropriate in a picture book, how children read them, everything she knew.

LSM: How else did you go about learning about picture book making?

RW: Watching Sid Caesar's *Your Show of Shows* and Jackie Gleason's *The Honeymooners* on television as a child had already taught me about comedy and timing. All of my books are tiny theater pieces, and you'll find that it was from those shows that I learned to do what I do.

Television was in its infancy and took its patterns and formats from the stage. Even the movies, musicals for instance, were conceived in a theatrical way, as if staged. My entire sense of language and of story and plot come from my father and from theater. That is how I think about my books.

LSM: During the late 1960s, Susan Hirschman and others were making a specialty of publishing picture books for very young children, and you yourself, from your early books onward, have often been drawn in that direction. Had the time somehow become right for this new focus?

RW: Very possibly, but I have no idea why. By then I had left Macmillan and had begun publishing with Phyllis Fogelman at Dial. Phyllis probably perceived an opening—a hole that needed to be filled—and moved right in to fill it. That is what the most creative people always do. A generation earlier, Margaret Wise Brown, who regarded children as people, had seen the possibility of an authentic literature for very young children. No one had ever attempted that before. Phyllis, as well, was part of Ursula's "charmed circle" at Harper, and she wanted to continue that tradition. As for myself, I don't think about the children who read my books. That is, I don't think about who my audience is going to be. I relate to children as individual human beings, not as a group or species! As I work, I simply think about the book itself.

LSM: When did you first think of yourself as a writer?

RW: I knew right away that, even though I was an illustrator, the stories were more important, and I wanted to do them. I was a far more accomplished and polished writer early on than I was an illustrator. It took me a long time before I was even a self-respecting artist, not just a loopy cartoonist. It took me twenty-five years to bring my art to the level of my writing.

We were talking earlier about childhood influences, and here I would like to make what I consider a crucial distinction. None of the actuality of what a writer or an artist is able to do has anything to do with childhood. Childhood affects subject matter. Those stories I choose to write, those subjects I choose to illustrate, have to do with experience, or with likes or dislikes that are conditioned. That's nurture. But talent is nature. Children's literature is practiced extremely well by a given number of people in every generation— maybe twenty in all. Talent is a gift from God. In my case, my writing talent is far greater than my drawing talent, which I have had to prune and school and develop.

LSM: *Benjamin and Tulip,* which is one of the first books you both wrote and illustrated, stands out as a far more raw book emotionally than are most books being published for young children today.

RW: It's about the way kids are. As a child you know who in your class is capable of pushing you around. Every child does. I don't ever try to put an adult happy face on childhood. This is one of the problems I have with adult political agendas being filtered into children's books—"everybody's happy together or at least everybody should be" themes, with no reality to them. The reason children have responded to *Benjamin and Tulip* is that in Benjamin they see Norman Buck, who used to wait after school for me and my best friend, Ginny O'Malley, and push us off our bicycles and roll us down the hill. There have always been bullies. This is childhood, and I try to write about it without prettying it up for grown-ups.

LSM: The late 1960s and early 1970s was a time of small picture books. Besides your own there were, for example, the very small books by Martha Alexander and Mercer Mayer. Did you enjoy working on that intimate scale? Why aren't more books like those being published now?

RW: I still love little books. They're for little hands, and children love them, too. But now most books are large because publishers want a book to serve as a poster for itself. They want it seen across a big store. They want a book that is a big presence.

LSM: You have often said that you based Ruby and Max on your two daughters, Victoria and Beezoo. Why, then, did you draw your characters as rabbits rather than as people?

RW: I always used animals. One reason is that animals are easier for me to draw. I have found it hard to draw really appealing children. Real children are very grubby and are not always nice to look at. So while I wouldn't want to idealize children, I also would not necessarily want to show them as they really are, either. And to go back to *Benjamin and Tulip,* that is a story about children pushing each other around. If I showed that happening between real children it wouldn't be publishable, and it wouldn't be funny. But with animals it becomes one step removed from reality and, therefore, acceptable.

LSM: Tell me about Angus, your first West Highland white terrier. You based some of your early animal characters on him, did you not—even animal characters that are not depicted as dogs?

RW: If you look at the bunnies or any of my other animal characters you'll see that they are all secretly West Highland white terriers, which are among the most expressive of dogs. Westies have ears that give you amazing signals and expressions. Their eyes and their body language are expressive, too. They're very dominant little dogs. If you get one, it trains you, you don't train it. Yet they are also very warm. They kiss you, and they talk to you endlessly!

LSM: Given your great affection for the dogs, why did you wait so long to make books that feature a West Highland white terrier, as you have in the *McDuff* series?

RW: If you go back to *Tell Me a Trudy* (1977) you'll find the first time I put a Westie in one of my books. But there are reasons why I didn't want to have a Westie character. Dogs don't fit into my world of soft, mystical bunnies. The bunnies live in their own world. Dogs are domesticated. Dogs are going to have a collar and a tag and a master.

LSM: Did you envision a board-book format for your first *Max and Ruby* stories right from the start?

RW: No, I didn't know what those stories were. To begin with, I simply thought of them as very short storybooks, meant to be sixteen pages long, or half the usual length of a picture book. I was thinking possibly of cloth books. It was Phyllis Fogelman at Dial who came up with the format we used. They became the very first board books with real stories and characters.

LSM: Why did you decide to reillustrate the *Max and Ruby* board books? What considerations were involved in remaking those books?

RW: I have also reillustrated *Noisy Nora* (1973; 1997), *Morris's Disappearing Bag* (1975; 1999), and *Timothy Goes to School* (1981; 2000). The considerations are about the same. You leave all the good parts but change what you could do better now. The pictures have changed because I'm a more sophisticated artist and have learned other techniques. And one thing I didn't want to happen is to have what I consider my life's best work in stories illustrated by a "less than her best" Rosemary Wells. Better to reillustrate them myself than to have somebody else come along and do so in fifty years' time. This was a particularly nice project—*Morris* and *Timothy*. I reillustrated them in 1999 with my new-old editor Regina Hayes at Viking. A very young Wells worked on the "original" *Morris* and *Timothy* with a very young Regina Hayes at Dial in the early seventies.

In *Max's Birthday* (1985; 1998), I changed the dragon in the original version to a lobster because I had done *Max's Dragon Shirt*

(1991) in the meantime and no longer found the dragon in the earlier book very convincing. If you look very carefully at the lobster, you'll see that he comes straight from the *Little Nemo* comic strip. I think the lobster is much funnier.

Max and Ruby are a lot bigger. The characters fill the page better. They have on their birthday clothing. Their actions are more anatomically believable if not exactly correct for made-up bunnies that are sort of bunnies and sort of West Highland white terriers. It's graphically more pleasing. The "around and around the lobster went" page is very decorative, which hadn't happened in a *Max* book before.

My way of working also changed. Back then I would first draw a character in pen line. The line and the expression would be all right, but they did not have very good definition because I had never been taught how to vary the thickness of the line, or about the beauty that comes of using line well. I would fill in the color and the background last. Now, I do the opposite. I take the page as a space. I put a little box around most of my drawings, which makes each one its own little world. And so I compose in that space, drawing the character first in pencil, then I go over it in very light blue pen. Then I color in everything, and only at the very last do I do the black line.

LSM: Tell me about your working relationship with Susan Jeffers. It goes back many years, does it not?

RW: I met Susan Jeffers in 1966 at Macmillan. We were both designers under Ava Weiss. Our collaborations can be explained by the fact that there are things that I can write, and that Susan can draw, that I can't draw. As Phyllis Fogelman, who was my editor at Dial for many years, once said, "Rosemary, everything you draw is funny." That is true. But not everything I write is funny, and so there have been times when I needed a different illustrator.

LSM: In an article called "The Artist at Work: The Writer at Work," which appeared in the March/April 1987 issue of *The Horn Book,* you stated that you were glad to have entered the field at a time when original writing was encouraged and retellings of classic stories were less emphasized. Has there been some change in the children's book field that has prompted you, in more recent years, to become more interested in retelling classic texts yourself?

RW: I still think I was lucky to come into the field when new writing was what publishers most wanted and when young artists and writers were given a lot of time to develop—six or seven books before their books were expected to sell. And I still think that retelling and reillustrating old stories is not a very important thing to do. I've done *Lassie Come-Home* and *Rachel Field's Hitty* (1999) and don't foresee doing any more.

Children's reading patterns had changed since the time those two books were first published. No one was reading *Lassie* or *Hitty* at all anymore. I felt the story of Lassie was a wonderful one about the loyalty of a dog and the absolutely terrific effort that an animal will make for love. *Hitty* was a great favorite of Susan Jeffers. I came to it late because I didn't like dolls as a child. Hitty is such a marvelous character, but some parts of the original book are racist, and we simply can't have any group of people in today's children's literature portrayed as superior or inferior to another group. The 1920s, '30s, and '40s was a time when nearly all children's books were written by educated, usually well-meaning white people, who were sympathetic to people of color but who sometimes expressed their attitudes patronizingly or in other ways that are simply no longer acceptable. And so to preserve *Hitty* at all, the book had to change. So I gave Hitty a variety of owners that accurately reflected American history, and I think I made them as real as Rachel Field would have done. It was not hard to write in Rachel Field's voice because my grandmother used to speak in exactly the way that Rachel Field writes. So I just recalled her voice, and it was great fun for me to do.

LSM: How did *My Very First Mother Goose* (1996) and *Here Comes Mother Goose* (1999), the two nursery rhyme collections edited by Iona Opie and illustrated by you, come about?

RW: Amy Ehrlich, the editor-in-chief of Candlewick Press, was another old friend from Dial. I had known Amy and worked with her on many of my best books. Amy asked me if I would do an enormous Mother Goose for them. At first I hesitated. I began to think of all the Mother Geese I knew. There would be a picture, the rhyme in maybe 14-point type, and the reader would keep turning the pages, on and on, and it just wasn't any fun. I didn't want to do that. But then I got into Mother Goose with Iona herself. Iona loves to say, "This is the Shakespeare of the kindergarten. This is the shortest great poetry of the language." She also says, "This is the greatest short poetry of the English language." With her help, I realized that Mother Goose rhymes are a gold mine of almost surreal, random poetry, that these are the words of our great-great-great-grandfathers and mothers, who were harnessmakers and shoemakers and milkmaids and farmers who didn't have radio or any books at all—just the handed-down, oral storytelling tradition. This was the poetry of real people who could not read or write but still had the English language at their command.

So I set aside everything else I was doing and took each poem and made a drawing without regard to size or format or the overall length of the book. And when I was done, I sent this pile of 165 paintings and sequences of paintings to Walker Books' designer, Amelia Edwards, who put them all together and made a book. She did it once, and she did it twice.

Among my favorites are the jump-rope rhymes because they come from the children themselves, and they're always the most fun. When children repeat something hundreds and hundreds of times, you know it's going to scan well, and there's not going to be an extra syllable. That kind of poetry is so completely rounded and beautiful that the sense of it doesn't matter. The rhythm and rhyme is everything that matters. This is one from the second book:

> Manchester Guardian,
> Evening News,
> Here comes a cat
> In high-heeled shoes.

It's wonderful because it has no relation to anything except its own logic.

LSM: It takes you out of this world.

RW: Yes, but at the same time this is very serious art. It's not "product."

LSM: Do you think that children today know Mother Goose rhymes to the same extent that they did when you were growing up?

RW: No. Everybody's in front of the TV. Childhood has changed in ways that scare me. When I was a child, kids were expected to organize their own games, and they did. Boys played pickup baseball. They organized their own teams. Maybe everything wasn't fair. But they did it. And girls played a lot of hopscotch and jump rope. We organized the games ourselves. The parents weren't interested. They didn't come around and say anything. And this is what we did because we didn't have television. Children had a world of their own making, and if it wasn't always fair it didn't matter because that's how it was, and they learned a lot from the experience. Adults didn't listen to their rhymes. Nobody cared. But now children's culture has been completely taken over by television. And so no, children don't know the old rhymes the way they used to. They know commercials instead. And they don't make up their own rhymes the way they used to, either.

One of the scariest aspects of all this is that commercial culture has taken over what I like to call the "popular crowd" or peer group. Everybody has to wear Gap clothes, or whatever the fad is, because television has taken over what's cool. It's not that you didn't have to be cool when I was growing up. Everybody wanted to be cool. But it wasn't quite so in your face or so early. Now there is very little childhood left. The more time that is spent in front of a screen, the less childhood. We're ending up with children who are well trained in materialism. And that is the reason I became involved in the "Read to Your Bunny" campaign, which is the first time I have ever been involved in any kind of public advocacy. The campaign—"The most important twenty minutes of the day are the twenty minutes you read to your child"—just came to me because of this. Children who don't have reading aloud experience with their parents on a regular basis are missing out on one of childhood's most important experiences.

LSM: I asked if you would bring along some books other than your own that you might want to talk about. What did you choose to bring?

RW: The first one, compiled as a catalog by Chris Beetles, is a compilation of artwork by an English watercolorist for children's books of the 1920s and '30s, Honor Appleton. Not many people have heard of Appleton, but I've learned enormously from her work. Her art is so toy-centered and so beautifully drawn. In *Here Comes Mother Goose* I drew upon Cecil Alden, Appleton, and the French artist Bernard Rabier, who was clearly an inspiration for Dr. Seuss.

The Doors of San Miguel de Allende is a book of photographs of doors found in a certain town in Mexico. I look at these photographs if I need to calm down at the end of the day. As I look at them, I sometimes also find architectural details that I need for my illustrations. But most of all, these pictures put me in a kind of meditative mood.

And here is a book called *Wheels: The Magical World of Automated Toys*. Many of the toys photographed in this book appear as real vehicles in my children's books—the yellow car driven by a cat, for instance, at the beginning of the "As I Was Going to St. Ives" chapter of *Here Comes Mother Goose*.

This is *The Friendly Book* by Welleran Poltarnees, who does marvelous compilations of art from historical children's books, which I love to pore over. And here is *French Trademarks of the Art Deco Era*, which I find just addictive. A book such as this gives me a sense of the world graphically from the time when I was young. And somehow trademarks and graphic symbols manage to become tiny but complete worlds in themselves. They would be enough—just one square inch of black-and-white art—to transport me as a child thousands of miles away. I had to learn the secret of that, and that's what I have been trying to do. Such images along with fabric designs and biscuit-tin labels and toys and dollhouse furniture and comic-strip art from the 1920s and 1930s are now a visual subtext in my work, especially in the Mother Goose books.

LSM: You seem to have used the Mother Goose books as a laboratory for experimenting with new techniques—collage, for instance, for the "Manchester Guardian" rhyme. And for the one that begins "Early in the morning at eight o'clock" you devised postage stamps for imaginary countries.

RW: Children love mail. I was fascinated with postage stamps when

I was little. I also make my own rubber stamps and stamp them all over my artwork now.

LSM: Why did the Mother Goose books in particular become the ones that prompted you to try so many new techniques and approaches?

RW: Because the rhymes are so wild and there is no narrative line or character I have to follow episodically, scene after scene. With Mother Goose I could, in a sense, relax.

LSM: Do you have a favorite among all your books?

RW: *Voyage to the Bunny Planet* (1992) is my favorite of all the books I have ever done. That set of three small books and *Mary on Horseback* are my best writing. By the time I had children, my mother lived next door to us in Westchester County, and I was able to see my childhood almost repeated through them. I could see how my mother affected my own children as she became like a second mother to them. She was such a free spirit, so pure in what she liked and disliked. I wanted to give my mother to the children in those three books—Claire and Felix and Robert—to have her give them the same huge comfort that I think she gave to my children.

But the Bunny Queen is really the mother of us all in heaven, coming down and pulling you away from the awful, blistered feet of the real world, and the socks running down into your shoes and the food you don't like to eat and the people who tease you and the fact that you can't do a cartwheel or that you're cold or hungry or not feeling well. The Bunny Queen is there to rescue you. They're really very meditative books. It's about the power of the mind to heal everything and transport the soul.

LSM: We seem somehow to have come back to that book of doors, which you said earlier also puts you in a meditative state of mind.

What exactly is it about the doors that you find comforting? Do you like to imagine what might be on the other side of the doors?

RW: Not really. The doorways are all possibilities, and there are eighty-five of them in the book. It is enough to see them, rather like being six years old and knowing your mother and father are asleep in their bed in the middle of a dark night. If you know they are there, you need not open the door.

·················

Charlotte Zolotow

Born June 26, 1915
Norfolk, Virginia

....

A *good picture book, Charlotte Zolotow once observed, "should help children understand the world better—their own inner conflicts, their own family, the things closest to them, problems they sometimes think belong only to them." In more than seventy picture books written with unwavering honesty, gentle humor, and a finely tuned lyricism, Zolotow has shown rare insight into the young child's point of view. Many of her stories focus on particular* aspects of friendship and family relationships—the envy of one classmate for another, the admiration of a younger sibling for an older one. As the titles of The Quarreling Book (1963) and William's Doll (1972) suggest, she has often ventured beyond the bounds of conventional subject matter for the very young, in the latter book challenging sexual stereotypes while making the sensible case that a caring attitude is as appropriate in boys as in girls. When Zolotow has written about nature, she has also done so out of an interest in relationships: the impact of a storm on the landscape and people in its path (The Storm Book, 1952), the accumulation of small details that add up to our sense of a season (Summer Is . . . 1967; 1983).*

Zolotow first entered the children's book field not as an author but as *secretary to Harper editor Ursula Nordstrom. She went on to have a distinguished publishing career of her own in parallel with her writing activities. Zolotow became editorial director of Harper Junior Books in 1976 and later founded her own Harper imprint, Charlotte Zolotow Books. Her authors over the years included Louise Fitzhugh, Paul Zindel, M. E. Kerr, Mary Rodgers, Robert Lipsyte, Patricia MacLachlan, Karla Kuskin, Paul Fleischman, and Francesca Lia Block.*

We recorded this interview at Zolotow's home north of New York City on October 23, 1998.

LEONARD S. MARCUS: Were books important to you as a child?

CHARLOTTE ZOLOTOW: Very, very important. I learned to read before I began school. In part because my family moved around a lot, I didn't have close friends until high school. Books became my life.

LSM: Where did your family live?

CZ: I was born in Norfolk, Virginia. When I was two, we moved to Detroit, but we returned to Virginia each year to visit my grandparents. Later, we moved to Brookline, Massachusetts, near Boston. Another new school! I didn't make friends easily. But in Brookline, I had a dog who was a dear friend. Pudgy was a Boston bullterrier. My first literary success was about her. She would walk me to school each morning and would always be there to meet me at the end of the school day. In fourth grade I wrote a theme about her, from the dog's point of view, that my teacher read out loud to the class. When I saw that she and the children all liked it, I suddenly realized that writing was a way to tell other people what was going on in my head. Until then, I hadn't thought anyone would be interested in anything I wanted to tell.

The following year, *American Girl* magazine ran a contest for readers. I sent in an essay about the little china dogs I collected and how they matched the dog characters in books I had read by Alfred Payson Terhune and others. I won a silver pencil for that theme. By then I also kept a diary in which I would write down everything I didn't want to tell anybody.

LSM: Would you tell me about your family?

CZ: My Southern mother was overprotective and believed that children should be seen and not heard. She was very elegant and loved beautiful clothes. My father was a lawyer and later tried to strike out in business for himself. He was a good lawyer but not a businessman. He loved working with his hands. While he was courting my mother, he had worked his way through law school by making fine quality reproductions of antique furniture. He built me a beautiful dollhouse furnished with tiny furniture. He loved to invent Rube Goldberg–looking things that were genuinely useful.

My older sister, Dorothy, always had friends—and lots of books at home. She gave me my two favorites, *Heidi* and *The Secret Garden,* both of which touched me deeply. I read *Heidi* over and over and cried so much that one day my mother asked my sister, "What kind of book is that child reading?"

LSM: Having been born in Virginia, did you consider yourself a Southerner?

CZ: No, but one of the things that alienated me from the children I met in Detroit was that I talked like a Southerner. I would say "you all" to two people and "yes, ma'am" and "no, ma'am" to teachers, which caused gales of laughter. In Boston, I had to learn to say "hahf" for "half" so the other children wouldn't laugh at the way I talked. When we moved to New York, everything I said sounded wrong. It was such a mixture of accents at first.

LSM: So you learned early on about being an outsider, which seems good preparation for a career in children's books.

CZ: Exactly. Once you've been an outsider, it's internalized.

LSM: Did you decide early on that you wanted to write?

CZ: Yes, but as a child I loved to draw as well as write. When asked what I wanted to be, I always said that I was going to be a writer and illustrate my own books.

LSM: What was school like for you?

CZ: By the time I reached junior high school we had moved to New York. I was fortunate to attend a new progressive school, called the Riverside School. Before that, I went to a public school in the city that was so crowded, children sat two to a seat. It was so noisy, the teacher spoke to us through a megaphone! In contrast to this impersonal situation, there were just four students in my Riverside graduating class. The teachers there were very understanding and encouraging and gave me a feeling of worth that was new to me. I didn't do well in many subjects, and I remember, for example, flunking a math exam and the teacher coming out and putting her arm around me and saying, "But Charlotte, I couldn't write a theme! Don't feel so badly."

LSM: What did you like to read at that time?

CZ: Poetry—Edna Millay and Elizabeth Browning. Along with poetry, I was especially interested in the short story. Katherine Mansfield was the writer I most wanted to be like. Her work has an immediacy that I later realized also comes into writing for children. To catch a moment and make it so vivid! And the emotion is what counted, not the plot. As an undergraduate at the University of Wisconsin at Madison, I studied with Helen C. White, and she praised me for my short stories. Some of them were read over the radio. So I was getting a sense that I had something to say through my writing. By then, I also loved the physical composition of books—the paper, the type, the design—as well as the writing and illustration.

LSM: After college, did you set out right away to begin your writing career?

cz: It was the time of the Great Depression, and I had to get a job. I found one at a bookstore, a Manhattan shop that specialized in American poetry. After about two weeks there, however, the owner tactfully suggested that I should spend less time reading the books and more time practicing my typing. Fortunately, there was an opening at Harper & Brothers just then. My sister, Dorothy, who worked there, alerted me to it.

lsm: Tell me about your first experiences at Harper and your first impressions of the house you came to be so closely associated with both as an author and editor.

cz: I knew that to start in publishing I needed a secretarial position, so I took shorthand (I couldn't do the diphthongs) and learned touch-typing. When I applied at Harper, I took a test given by a lady named Marianne Brindwell and proceeded to flunk it. Miss Brindwell told me I hadn't passed and then said—imagine anyone doing this today—"Dear, I think you're nervous. Why don't you come back tomorrow and try again." So I did return and was able to transcribe her dictation. And so I was given a job in the adult trade department entering and returning manuscripts. My sister already knew Ursula Nordstrom, who had begun her career at Harper in the college department. My sister worked in the high school department. They were the same age. Now I began to know Ursula, too, and when Ursula took over Harper's Department of Books for Boys and Girls from Louise Raymond, she invited me out to lunch. I had read [the Swiss psychologist Jean] Piaget in college, and I remember carrying on with Ursula about how adults didn't show enough respect for children. I told her I thought Harper's should publish a volume for children of Emily Dickinson's poems. No book of that kind had yet been done. Ursula didn't publish the book, but she liked my attitude about children. I loved the children's book department because it combined the art I loved—the visual and physical qualities of the book—with literature. So when Ursula offered me a job I was delighted.

LSM: What did you do as Ursula Nordstrom's assistant?

CZ: There were just three of us in the department then: Ursula, me, and a secretary. I did just about everything, including some typing and answering the telephone. It was also part of my job to meet writers and artists at the elevator and screen the new ones who came wanting to show their work. I remember the time I went back to tell Ursula, "There's a strange lady out there with a strange idea. But she has a fantastic mind and I think you should meet her." That was Ruth Krauss. The idea she had come to present was for a picture book about Adolf Hitler.

After a while I was writing flap copy. Then Ursula began giving me manuscripts to read, and by and by I became what was called a "reader." I later became an assistant editor, then a full editor, then associate publisher of a, by then, much larger children's book department, and finally, now, publisher emerita.

LSM: How did your own first children's book, *The Park Book* (1944), come about?

CZ: In college, I wrote some stories from the point of view of a child. That, in a sense, was a beginning. By the time I was working at Harper's, my husband and I were living near Washington Square Park, in New York's Greenwich Village. I didn't have children then but, nonetheless, had learned the whole cycle of daily life in the park, starting with early morning when people were hurrying off to work, followed by children going to school, then by mothers with their small children, and so on. It was the continuous cycle that seized me, the fact that each time a new group came along it completely changed the park's personality. Margaret Wise Brown was, of course, still alive and writing new books every year. I adored her work, and so I wrote a long memo about the park to Ursula, sug-

WAYS OF TELLING

• 220

gesting that it would make an ideal subject for Margaret Wise Brown. I put my memo on Ursula's desk, and when she'd read it she came over to me and, sounding sort of irritated, said, "I don't know what you mean. What do you mean by this?" And I said, "Well, just that it keeps changing completely. . . ." To which she replied, "Well, how does it change?" So I wrote down more of my observations and gave my memo back to Ursula, still thinking of it as a good idea for Margaret. This time when Ursula came over to me, her tone of voice had completely changed. She said, "Congratulations! You've just written your first children's book!" Then she went on, "You must never, ever, ever tell a writer what you think would make a wonderful book. The idea has to come from the writer. What you have here is *your* book, not Margaret's." So in that one explanation, Ursula taught me about being an editor and about being a writer. It was a tremendous piece of education that has lasted for the rest of my life.

LSM: H. A. Rey, who was living on Washington Square during the 1940s, illustrated *The Park Book*. What did you think of his illustrations?

CZ: I had originally imagined very poetic, sensitive illustrations by Leonard Weisgard and was upset at first with the choice! But Ursula was right: Rey's illustrations broke the seriousness of the text for kids and contributed what I call the visual subplot of the book. For example, I described the people going to work in the morning and coming home at night, looking tired. In the illustrations for those scenes, Rey put in wastebaskets that were empty in the morning and full in the evening. Visual details such as that gave a lively reality to the book.

LSM: *The Park Book* is unusual for not having a plot.

CZ: A lot of my books don't! I wrote mood books before I had children. It was the mood I wanted to get across to children. Moods are

Charlotte Zolotow

important in a child's life. Playing alone as I did as a child and always observing, my responses to the changing seasons, for example, were very intense. I knew that there were a great many children who would also respond, if only a writer could catch it for them in a book.

LSM: At the time you wrote *The Park Book,* what in particular did you admire about Margaret Wise Brown's work? Do you feel the same way about her books now?

CZ: I do. For one thing, there is the sound of her words. You would want to hear *Goodnight Moon* even if the language it is written in was foreign to you. I think also that Margaret had known some of the same kinds of experiences in life that led to intense awareness of mood and emotion and to a love of nature. Margaret had more humor than I do. There is a more suppressed humor in my books, but people don't think of me as very funny, though many of my books are subtly so.

Margaret was very kind to me when I was Ursula's secretary. We didn't have air-conditioning at Harper then, and during the summer months the office was hot as hell. Margaret would come in to see Ursula with three ice-cold Coca-Colas all frosted on the outside, as a treat for the three of us in that very hot office.

LSM: You spoke before of your childhood ambition to illustrate the books you would write one day. As a newly published writer, did you still have some such aspirations? Did you consider the possibility of illustrating your picture books?

CZ: Several years after *The Park Book* was published, when Ursula was having a terrible time finding an artist for *Three Funny Friends* (1961), I did some drawings myself to show how I saw it. I showed them to Ursula. She didn't like them. It was really botanical illustration that I was best at. I still do some painting. When I'm outside, especially in the fall, or in the garden, I want to paint what I see and feel.

LSM: Many authors have an especially hard time writing their second book. Did you have that experience following the publication of *The Park Book*?

CZ: Not exactly, no. By the time I wrote my second book, *But Not Billy* (1947), I had become a mother. I hadn't been around babies much up until then, and so every time Steve did something new—like open his eyes!—I was amazed. That total amazement at the funny poses that babies strike as they grow found their way into that book. I was leaving mood behind and becoming fascinated by the changes that a baby goes through. Steve was a revelation!

I took to being a mother wholeheartedly. With a baby to care for, it was very hard to find time to write. I was involved, too, with my husband's career. Maurice wrote about the movies and Broadway— he was known as the "Boswell of Broadway"—and I did some secretarial work for him. My world was so divided. By and by the only quiet time I had to myself was when Steve, and later also his sister, Ellen, were napping. I also had cooking and other household work to do. We didn't have a washing machine in our New York apartment, and whenever I went down to the basement of our building to do the wash, I brought along my pad and pencil and would write while the laundry was spinning around. Those were the sort of stolen moments I made for writing.

LSM: At Harper, did you and Ursula and the others who later joined you in the department think in terms of "experimental" books? Is that how you might have described the kinds of books you were eager to publish?

CZ: No. I would say rather that we simply looked for books that gripped us. We began by falling in love with the text. We thought that a good picture book text had to first stand on its own without pictures.

We certainly weren't interested in trends. Ursula always said that

Charlotte Zolotow

she could never have gone out and looked for "a Maurice Sendak." You had to see that something about a work was compelling, and then you had to believe in it even when other people laughed or objected, as some people did at the beginning.

Later, when *William's Doll* was about to be published, Ursula presented the book at a sales conference, and the salesmen, some of them hard-boiled guys, made a fuss. They said, "Cut down the printing on this one! We'll never sell it. Who's going to buy a book about a boy with a doll?" But Ursula had the guts to stand up to the men and not reduce the printing. It did take guts, because many of the books she stood up for in that way didn't succeed.

LSM: What was it like to work as an editor, as you did for many years, while also writing books of your own?

CZ: Schizophrenic! Often I would read a picture book manuscript that was almost right and would see exactly how I would like to fix it. Had I made the revisions, however, it would have become my book, and so I had to resist the temptation and go back to the author and ask him or her to fix where it didn't work. An editor who revises a manuscript may (or may not) get a better book but destroy the writer's own vision.

LSM: *The Storm Book* is another very unusual picture book. It, too, has no plot, and the one child who appears in it is really a minor character compared with the forces of nature. How did you structure this storyless book? What accounts for its considerable drama?

CZ: Storms are dramatic. I always loved rain and thunder and lightning. One of the short stories I wrote in college concerned a storm as seen from a child's point of view. And later there was a little girl who lived in our building in Washington Square who was scared to death of thunderstorms. I remember once saying to her, "But it's so beautiful! Look at the lovely blue color of the lightning," and so on. That experience probably set me off. I was also fascinated by the fact that a storm could be experienced differently by people in the city than it was experienced by others at the seashore or in the country.

LSM: So the storm became an occasion for writing about the connections between people as well as about their different points of view. Those two themes lie at the core of many of your books, do they not?

CZ: Oh, yes! They are often about connections and the cycles of the seasons and of life. A lot of my books are also about friendship. The possibility of getting in another person's head and seeing the world from that other person's point of view is one of the fascinations that writing has had for me since childhood.

LSM: In your book, the storm seems almost comforting. However fearsome, it is the one thing that binds all the people and places together.

CZ: You are very perceptive! I think I'm a pantheist at heart.

LSM: Several of your books are also unusual for having surprisingly tentative endings.

CZ: It's something I feel very keenly. We don't know how anything in life is going to come out; often there is no definite right or wrong in a situation. In *A Father Like That* (1971), for instance, a child fantasizes about the kind of father he would like to have. All through the book, the little boy dreams up a wonderful father. Then, at the very end, the mother says, well, in case you never do have a father like that, you can grow up and be one yourself. Rather than providing a conventional happy ending, you see, the mother's final comment leaves the situation open-ended, as in fact it is going to be for so many children who live in single-parent households. It offers hope but not a promise.

LSM: *If You Listen* (1980) also concerns a child at home and an absent father. In this book, a resourceful and sympathetic mother

Charlotte Zolotow

225 •

suggests a variety of ways for her lonely child to imagine, or possibly even feel, the father's presence.

CZ: I call that my Zen book. The sounds of trains at night or of distant church bells, for instance, can give one a feeling of connection with a faraway loved person. It's mystical! I have had this experience and know that it is possible.

LSM: At the end of the book, however, you put everything into question. The child, as if shrugging off all his mother's suggestions, says to her, "But I wish he'd come home."

CZ: Yes, well this is one of the ways that a child would feel. But at least the story gives the child something to fall back on, even though he can't stop missing the person.

LSM: Many of your books concern the intense feelings associated with friendship. In *It's Not Fair* (1976), you write about two friends who envy each other, and show that even someone who appears to "have everything" may in fact not be happy at all.

CZ: It's life: Life isn't fair, and if kids see that, they'll be better able to cope by balancing the good and bad in each other's life.

I based *The New Friend* (1968; 1981) on an adult experience of a friend of mine, who was heartbroken when her best friend went off with somebody else. The book ends with the narrator saying, "Someday I'll find a new friend." Perhaps. But it's never going to be the same, and children know that, too.

In writing, I often start with an emotion drawn from adult experience and translate it into a story for children. I remember talking with Ursula in the office one day about someone who had made me furious. Ursula said, "You shouldn't let all this good anger go to waste!" And so I went home and wrote *The Unfriendly Book* (1975).

LSM: Did the feminist movement of the 1970s influence your work in any particular way?

CZ: Feminism began before the 1970s. I was a feminist way back.

The early women writers were all feminists, not politically, but emotionally. George Eliot for one. This was part of the background of *William's Doll*. So many men of that era felt that women belonged at home, taking care of the housekeeping and the children. I was in Washington Square Park one day when I overheard a little boy telling his parents that he wanted a doll, and the father's response was: "Get him a gun instead!" His mother shook her head and looked over at me.

LSM: Do you find it interesting to revise your books, as you have done on occasion, for a later edition? What prompts you to make these changes?

CZ: I'll make revisions when some detail in a book has become outdated. In *One Step, Two* (1955; 1981), for instance, which is one of my favorite books, I described a hurdy-gurdy man with a monkey and mentioned the rattle of milk bottles in the milkwagon. I took out these details in the later edition because today's children would no longer recognize them from their own experience and might be confused. Times change, but not the moods I write about. Often, though, the minute I see the printed version of any new book of mine, I find something I wish I had written a little differently, a little better.

LSM: Tell me about the revised ending of *A Rose, a Bridge, and a Wild Black Horse* (1964; 1987). Does the new ending, in which the younger sister goes off with her brother to explore the world instead of staying behind, show the influence of feminism?

CZ: That's interesting because I thought of the original version of that book as feminist. I had intended for the ending to be read ironically; here was all this tight companionship between the brother and sister and then at the very last moment he simply goes off by himself. I wanted readers to feel the unfairness of that. I felt, at first, that readers who said that the girl should also explore the world had read the story in too literal-minded a way. But I was also able to see their point of view and so I later changed my mind, and I changed the ending to their going off together.

LSM: *My Grandson Lew* (1974), like *William's Doll,* touches on a subject that at the time was considered taboo, or near-taboo, in books for younger children: the death of a loved one. What prompted you to write that book?

CZ: The grandfather character is a composite of several sweet people I knew who were very good to children. The story itself grew out of a number of experiences. When my own grandfather died in Norfolk, we were living in Brookline, and nobody told me that he had died. I hadn't been very close to him but, still, nobody told me. And then I saw my mother crying and noticed various people not acting as they usually did, and still nobody said anything. By and by I began to piece together the fact that my grandfather wasn't coming to visit anymore with all the unusual behavior I had observed, and that was how I realized, finally, that he was dead.

The book also recalls my father-in-law's relationship with my son, Steve. But it draws most directly on my feelings of fondness for an aunt of mine, who had just died when I wrote the book. I had gone down for the funeral and come back and was sitting on the porch at home with my daughter, who was six or seven. I was teaching Ellen how to crochet, and she was having trouble getting the thing going. And I remember that I was abstracted, which was unlike me. I usually entered into whatever was going on with the children. Finally, Ellen said, "How come you're so crazy about this aunt? I never met her or even heard about her." I then began trying to describe my aunt but couldn't find any way of making her real for Ellen. Then suddenly it hit me, and I said, "She was the one who taught me how to crochet." And with that my Aunt Ann came alive for Ellen, too (connections again). So what mainly set me off writing *My Grand-*

son Lew was the realization that talking about a dead person can, in a sense, bring that person back to life. I loved talking about my aunt to Ellen and knowing that I had made her real for my daughter.

LSM: The mother and child in your story each tells something about the grandfather that the other didn't know before.

CZ: That's right. They fill out the story for each other. But it was Ellen's asking the question that set me off.

LSM: As an editor you have published novels by Louise Fitzhugh, M. E. Kerr, Paul Zindel, Francesca Lia Block, and a great many others. Have you ever considered writing a novel yourself?

CZ: No, because the thing that impels me is always one solid, intense emotion. A novel to me is so vast. I've started but not finished them.

LSM: Would you tell me about some of the letters you have received from children?

CZ: Some letters are just funny: "We had to write to an author, and I got you." But I have also received beautiful and sometimes heartbreaking letters from children, including one about *The Hating Book* (1969) from a little girl who wrote, "How did you know about me and my friend?" Those are the letters that have touched me the most—the ones that say, "How did you know about me?"—because that means I've really connected my experience with theirs.

....

Bibliography

MITSUMASA ANNO

Anno's Alphabet. New York: Crowell, 1975.

Anno's Counting Book. New York: Crowell, 1975.

Anno's Journey. New York: Philomel, 1977.

Anno's Math Games. New York: Philomel, 1987.

Anno's Math Games II. New York: Philomel, 1989.

Anno's Math Games III. New York: Philomel, 1991.

Anno's Medieval World. New York: Philomel, 1980.

Anno's Mysterious Multiplying Jar, by Masaichiro Anno. New York: Philomel, 1983.

Anno's U.S.A. New York: Philomel, 1983.

Topsy-Turvies: Pictures to Stretch the Imagination. New York: Weatherhill, 1970.

ASHLEY BRYAN

I Greet the Dawn: Poems, by Paul Laurence Dunbar. New York: Atheneum, 1978.

Moon, For What Do You Wait? by Rabindranath Tagore. New York: Atheneum, 1967.

The Dancing Granny. New York: Atheneum, 1977.

The Night Has Ears: African Proverbs. New York: Atheneum, 1999.

The Ox of the Wonderful Horns and Other African Folktales, edited by Richard Lewis. New York: Atheneum, 1971.

The Sun Is So Quiet, by Nikki Giovanni. New York: Atheneum, 1996.

Turtle Knows Your Name. New York: Atheneum, 1989.

Walk Together Children. New York: Atheneum, 1974.

ERIC CARLE

A House for Hermit Crab. New York: Simon & Schuster, 1988.

Brown Bear, Brown Bear, What Do You See? by Bill Martin Jr. New York: Holt, Rinehart & Winston, 1983.

Draw Me a Star. New York: Philomel, 1992.

Flora and Tiger: 19 Very Short Stories from My Life. New York: Philomel, 1997.

Hello, Red Fox. New York: Simon & Schuster, 1998.

1, 2, 3 to the Zoo. New York: World, 1968.

Rooster's Off to See the World. New York: Simon & Schuster, 1987.

The Art of Eric Carle. New York: Philomel, 1996.

The Mixed-Up Chameleon. New York: Crowell, 1975.

The Very Hungry Caterpillar. New York: Collins World, 1969.

The Very Quiet Cricket. New York: Philomel, 1990.

Today Is Monday. New York: Philomel, 1993.

T A N A   H O B A N

Little Elephant, by Miela Ford. New York: Greenwillow, 1994.

Look Again! New York: Macmillan, 1971.

Look Book. New York: Greenwillow, 1997.

More, Fewer, Less. New York: Greenwillow, 1998.

Of Colors and Things. New York: Greenwillow, 1989.

Shapes and Things. New York: Macmillan, 1970.

The Moon Was the Best, by Charlotte Zolotow. New York: Greenwillow, 1993.

26 Letters and 99 Cents. New York: Greenwillow, 1987.

K A R L A   K U S K I N

In the Middle of the Trees. New York: Harper, 1958.

James and the Rain. New York: Harper, 1957.

Jerusalem, Shining Still, illustrated by David Frampton. New York: Harper, 1987.

Just Like Everyone Else. New York: Harper, 1959.

Near the Window Tree: Poems and Notes. New York: Harper, 1975.

Roar and More. New York: Harper, 1956.

Soap Soup and Other Verses. New York: HarperCollins, 1992.

The Bear Who Saw the Spring. New York: Harper, 1961.

The Dallas Titans Get Ready for Bed, illustrated by Marc Simont. New York: Harper, 1986.

The Philharmonic Gets Dressed, illustrated by Marc Simont. New York: Harper, 1982.

The Rose on My Cake. New York: Harper, 1964.
The Sky Is Always in the Sky. New York: HarperCollins, 1998.

J A M E S   M A R S H A L L
Fox on the Job. New York: Dial, 1988.
George and Martha. Boston: Houghton Mifflin, 1972.
Goldilocks and the Three Bears. New York: Dial, 1988.
Hansel and Gretel. New York: Dial, 1990.
Plink, Plink, Plink, by Byrd Baylor. Boston: Houghton Mifflin, 1971.
Red Riding Hood. New York: Dial, 1987.

R O B E R T   M c C L O S K E Y
Blueberries for Sal. New York: Viking, 1948.
Homer Price. New York: Viking, 1943.
Lentil. New York: Viking, 1940.
Make Way for Ducklings. New York: Viking, 1941.
One Morning in Maine. New York: Viking, 1952.
Time of Wonder. New York: Viking, 1957.

I O N A   O P I E
A Nursery Companion, co-edited by Peter Opie. New York: Oxford, 1980.
Tail Feathers from Mother Goose: The Opie Rhyme Book, co-edited by
    Peter Opie. Boston: Little, Brown, 1988.
The Lore and Language of Schoolchildren, co-authored by Peter Opie.
    New York: Oxford, 1959.
The Oxford Book of Children's Verse, co-edited by Peter Opie. New York:
    Oxford, 1973.
The Oxford Dictionary of Nursery Rhymes, co-edited by Peter Opie.
    New York: Oxford, 1951.

H E L E N   O X E N B U R Y
Clap Hands. New York: Macmillan, 1987.
Dressing. New York: Simon & Schuster, 1981.
Eating Out. New York: Dial, 1983.
Numbers of Things. New York: Franklin Watts, 1967.

The Birthday Party. New York: Dial, 1983.

The Car Trip. New York: Dial, 1983.

We're Going on a Bear Hunt, by Michael Rosen. New York: Margaret K. McElderry Books, 1989.

Working. New York: Simon & Schuster, 1981.

JERRY PINKNEY

Aesop's Fables. New York: SeaStar, 2000.

Black Cowboy, Wild Horses, by Julius Lester. New York: Dial, 1998.

John Henry, by Julius Lester. New York: Dial, 1994.

Journeys with Elijah, by Barbara Diamond Goldin. San Diego: Harcourt Brace, 1999.

Minty, by Alan Schroeder. New York: Dial, 1996.

Mirandy and Brother Wind, by Patricia C. McKissack. New York: Knopf, 1988.

Rabbit Makes a Monkey Out of Lion, by Verna Aardema. New York: Dial, 1989.

Sam and the Tigers, by Julius Lester. New York: Dial, 1996.

The Hired Hand, by Robert D. San Souci. New York: Dial, 1997.

The Little Match Girl, adapted from Hans Christian Andersen. New York: Phyllis Fogelman Books, 1999.

The Patchwork Quilt, by Valerie Flournoy. New York: Dial, 1985.

The Ugly Duckling, adapted from Hans Christian Andersen. New York: Morrow Junior Books, 1999.

MAURICE SENDAK

A Hole Is to Dig, by Ruth Krauss. New York: Harper, 1952.

A Very Special House, by Ruth Krauss. New York: Harper, 1953.

Dear Mili, by Wilhelm Grimm. New York: Farrar, Straus, and Giroux, 1988.

Hector Protector and As I Went Over the Water. New York: Harper, 1965.

Higglety Pigglety Pop! New York: Harper, 1967.

In the Night Kitchen. New York: Harper, 1970.

I Saw Esau: The Schoolchild's Pocket Book, edited by Iona and Peter Opie. Cambridge, MA: Candlewick, 1992.

Outside Over There. New York: Harper, 1981.

We Are All in the Dumps with Jack and Guy. New York: HarperCollins, 1993.
Where the Wild Things Are. New York: Harper, 1963.

WILLIAM STEIG

A Gift from Zeus, by Jeanne Steig. New York: Harper, 2001.
A Handful of Beans, by Jeanne Steig. New York: HarperCollins, 1998.
Amos & Boris. New York: Farrar, Straus, and Giroux, 1971.
C D B! New York: Windmill, 1968.
Consider the Lemming, by Jeanne Steig. New York:
   Farrar, Straus, and Giroux, 1988.
Doctor De Soto. New York: Farrar, Straus, and Giroux, 1982.
Farmer Palmer's Wagon Ride. New York: Farrar, Straus, and Giroux, 1974.
Roland the Minstrel Pig. New York: Windmill, 1968.
Shrek! New York: Farrar, Straus, and Giroux, 1990.
Spinky Sulks. New York: Farrar, Straus, and Giroux, 1988.
Sylvester and the Magic Pebble. New York: Windmill, 1969.
The Amazing Bone. New York: Farrar, Straus, and Giroux, 1976.
The Lonely Ones. New York: Duell, Sloan and Pearce, 1942.
The Real Thief. New York: Farrar, Straus, and Giroux, 1973.
Tiffky Doofky. New York: Farrar, Straus, and Giroux, 1978.
Zeke Pippin. New York: HarperCollins, 1994.

ROSEMARY WELLS

Benjamin and Tulip. New York: Dial, 1973.
Here Comes Mother Goose, edited by Iona Opie. Cambridge, MA:
   Candlewick, 1999.
Lassie Come-Home, illustrated by Susan Jeffers. New York: Holt, 1995.
Mary on Horseback: Three Mountain Stories, illustrated by Peter McCarty.
   New York: Dial, 1998.
Max's Birthday. New York: Dial, 1985, 1998.
Max's Dragon Shirt. New York: Dial, 1991.
Morris's Disappearing Bag. New York: Dial, 1975; New York: Viking, 1999.
My Very First Mother Goose, edited by Iona Opie. Cambridge, MA:
   Candlewick, 1996.
Noisy Nora. New York: Dial, 1973; 1999.

Bibliography

Rachel Field's Hitty: Her First Hundred Years, illustrated by Susan Jeffers.
New York: Simon & Schuster, 1999.
Tell Me a Trudy, by Lore Segal. New York: Farrar, Straus, and Giroux, 1977.
Through the Hidden Door. New York: Dial, 1987.
Timothy Goes to School. New York: Dial, 1981; New York: Viking, 2000.
Voyage to the Bunny Planet. New York: Viking, 1992.

CHARLOTTE ZOLOTOW
A Father Like That, illustrated by Ben Shecter. New York: Harper, 1971.
A Rose, a Bridge, and a Wild Black Horse, illustrated by Uri Shulevitz.
New York: Harper, 1964; re-illustrated by Robin Spowart. New York:
Harper, 1987.
But Not Billy, illustrated by Lys Cassal. New York: Harper, 1947;
re-illustrated by Kay Chorao. Harper, 1983.
If You Listen, illustrated by Marc Simont. New York: Harper, 1980.
It's Not Fair, illustrated by William Pène du Bois. New York: Harper, 1976.
My Grandson Lew, illustrated by William Pène du Bois. New York:
Harper, 1974.
One Step, Two . . . , illustrated by Roger Duvoisin. New York: Lothrop, 1955.
Summer Is . . . , illustrated by Janet Archer. New York: Abelard-Schuman,
1967; re-illustrated by Ruth Lercher Bornstein. New York: Crowell, 1967.
The Hating Book, illustrated by Ben Shecter. New York: Harper, 1969.
The New Friend, illustrated by Arvis L. Stewart. New York:
Abelard-Schuman, 1968; re-illustrated by Emily A. McCully.
New York: Crowell, 1981.
The Park Book, illustrated by H. A. Rey. New York: Harper, 1944.
The Quarreling Book, illustrated by Arnold Lobel. New York: Harper, 1963.
The Storm Book, illustrated by Margaret Bloy Graham. New York:
Harper, 1952.
The Unfriendly Book, illustrated by William Pène du Bois. New York:
Harper, 1975.
Three Funny Friends. New York: Harper, 1961.
William's Doll, illustrated by William Pène du Bois. New York: Harper, 1972.

Photo Credits

Page 7: courtesy of Ann K. Beneduce; page 18: photo by Matthew Wysocki, reproduced by permission of Ashley Bryan; page 32: photo by Stephen Petegorsky, reproduced by permission of Eric Carle; page 58: photo by Meila Ford, reproduced by permission of Meila Ford; page 68: photo by Nick Kuskin, courtesy of Karla Kuskin; page 82: reproduced by permission of Penguin Putnam Inc; page 106: photo by Elaine S. Martens, reproduced by permission of Elaine S. Martens; page 117: reproduced by permission of Gloucestershire Media; page 141: reproduced by permission of Candlewick Press; page 150: photo by Gordon Trice, reproduced by permission of Gordon Trice; page 165: © Chris Callis, reproduced by permission of Chris Callis Studio; page 182: photo by Nancy Crampton, reproduced by permission of Nancy Crampton; page 197: photo by Carolyn Ebbitt, reproduced by permission of Penguin Putnam Inc.; page 215: photo by Andrew Kilgore, reproduced by permission of HarperCollins.

Illustration Credits

Mitsumasa Anno

Anno's Alphabet: An Adventure in Imagination: Copyright © 1974 by Fukuinkan Shoten. Used by permission of HarperCollins Publishers.

Anno's Journey: From *Anno's Journey* by Mitsumasa Anno, copyright © 1977 by Mitsumasa Anno. Translation copyright © 1978 by Fukuinkan Shoten Publishers. Used by permission of Philomel Books, an imprint of Penguin Putnam Books for Young Readers, a division of Penguin Putnam Inc. All rights reserved.

Ashley Bryan

The Story of the Three Kingdoms: Illustrations copyright © 1995 by Ashley Bryan; text copyright © 1995 by Walter Dean Myers. Used by permission of HarperCollins Publishers.

The Dancing Granny: Reprinted with the permission of Atheneum Books for Young Readers, an imprint of Simon & Schuster Children's Publishing Division, from *The Dancing Granny* by Ashley Bryan. Copyright © 1977 Ashley Bryan.

Eric Carle

The Very Hungry Caterpillar: From *The Very Hungry Caterpillar*. Copyright © 1969 and 1987 by Eric Carle. All rights reserved.

The Very Quiet Cricket: From *The Very Quiet Cricket*. Copyright © 1990 by Eric Carle. All rights reserved.

Brown Bear, Brown Bear, What Do You See?: From *Brown Bear, Brown Bear, What Do You See?* by Bill Martin Jr. Illustrated by Eric Carle. Images copyright © 1983 by Eric Carle. All rights reserved. Text copyright © 1967, renewed 1995 by Bill Martin Jr., reproduced by permission of the publisher, Henry Holt, New York.

Tana Hoban

Count and See: Reprinted with the permission of Simon & Schuster Books for Young Readers, an imprint of Simon & Schuster Children's Publishing Division, from *Count and See* by Tana Hoban. Copyright © 1972 Tana Hoban.

Exactly the Opposite: Copyright © 1990 by Tana Hoban. Used by permission of HarperCollins Publishers.

Karla Kuskin

The Philharmonic Gets Dressed: Illustrations copyright © 1982 by Marc Simont; text copyright © 1982 by Karla Kuskin. Used by permission of HarperCollins Publishers.

Roar and More: Copyright © 1956, renewed 1990 by Karla Kuskin. Reprinted by permission of Scott Treimel New York.

James Marshall

Goldilocks and the Three Bears: From *Goldilocks and the Three Bears* by James Marshall, copyright © 1988 by James Marshall. Used by permission of Dial Books for Young Readers, an imprint of Penguin Putnam Books for Young Readers, a division of Penguin Putnam Inc. All rights reserved.

Miss Nelson Has a Field Day: Illustration from *Miss Nelson Has a Field Day* by Harry Allard and James Marshall. Copyright © 1985 by James Marshall. Reprinted by permission of Houghton Mifflin Company. All rights reserved.

Robert McCloskey

Make Way for Ducklings: From *Make Way for Ducklings* by Robert McCloskey, copyright 1941, renewed © 1969 by Robert McCloskey. Used by permission of Viking Penguin, an imprint of Penguin Putnam Books for Young Readers, a division of Penguin Putnam Inc. All rights reserved.

One Morning in Maine: From *One Morning in Maine* by Robert McCloskey, copyright 1952, renewed © 1980 by Robert McCloskey. Used by permission of Viking Penguin, an imprint of Penguin Putnam Books for Young Readers, a division of Penguin Putnam Inc. All rights reserved.

Helen Oxenbury

Eating Out: From *Eating Out* by Helen Oxenbury, copyright © 1983 Helen Oxenbury. Reproduced by permission of Walker Books Limited, London.

We're Going on a Bear Hunt: (U.S.): Reprinted with the permission of Margaret K. McElderry Books, an imprint of Simon & Schuster Children's Publishing Division, from *We're Going on a Bear Hunt* by Michael Rosen, illustrated by Helen Oxenbury. Text copyright © 1989 Michael Rosen. Illustrations © 1989 Helen Oxenbury. (Canada): *We're Going on a Bear Hunt* Text © 1989 Michael Rosen. Illustrations © 1989 Helen Oxenbury. Reproduced by permission of Walker Books Limited, London.

Jerry Pinkney

John Henry: From *John Henry* by Julius Lester, illustrated by Jerry Pinkney, copyright © 1994 by Jerry Pinkney, illustrations. Used by permission of Dial Books for Young Readers, an imprint of Penguin Putnam Books for Young Readers, a division of Penguin Putnam Inc. All rights reserved.

The Talking Eggs: From *The Talking Eggs* by Robert D. San Souci, pictures by Jerry Pinkney, copyright © 1989 by Jerry Pinkney, pictures. Used by permission of Dial Books for Young Readers, an imprint of Penguin Putnam Books for Young Readers, a division of Penguin Putnam Inc. All rights reserved.

Maurice Sendak

A Hole Is to Dig: A First Book of First Definitions: Text copyright 1952 by Ruth Krauss. Text copyright renewed 1980 by Ruth Krauss. Illustrations copyright 1952 by Maurice

239 •

Sendak. Illustrations copyright renewed 1980 by Maurice Sendak. All rights reserved.

In the Night Kitchen: Copyright © 1970 by Maurice Sendak. All rights reserved. Lettering by Diana Blair. Twenty-fifth Anniversary Edition. HarperCollins Publishers.

I Saw Esau: The Schoolchild's Pocket Book: Text copyright © 1992 by Iona Opie; illustrations copyright © 1992 by Maurice Sendak. Reproduced by permission of the publisher, Candlewick Press, Inc., Cambridge, MA., on behalf of Walker Books Limited, London.

William Steig

Brave Irene and *Doctor De Soto:*

Reprinted by permission of Farrar, Straus and Giroux, LLC:

Illustration from *Brave Irene* by William Steig. Copyright © 1986 by William Steig.

Illustration from *Doctor De Soto* by William Steig. Copyright © 1982 by William Steig.

Rosemary Wells

Noisy Nora: From *Noisy Nora (Original Edition)* by Rosemary Wells, copyright © 1973 by Rosemary Wells. Used by permission of Dial Books for Young Readers, an imprint of Penguin Putnam Books for Young Readers, a division of Penguin Putnam Inc. All rights reserved.

Noisy Nora: From *Noisy Nora (With All New Illustrations)* by Rosemary Wells, copyright © 1973 by Rosemary Wells, text. Copyright © 1997 by Rosemary Wells, illustrations. Used by permission of Dial Books for Young Readers, an imprint of Penguin Putnam Books for Young Readers, a division of Penguin Putnam Inc. All rights reserved.

My Very First Mother Goose: Text copyright © 1996 by Iona Opie; illustrations copyright © 1996 by Rosemary Wells. Reproduced by permission of the publisher, Candlewick Press, Inc., Cambridge, MA.

Charlotte Zolotow

The Storm Book: Illustrations copyright © 1952 by Margaret Bloy Graham. Used by permission of HarperCollins Publishers.

William's Doll: Pictures copyright © 1972 by William Pène du Bois. Text copyright © 1972 by Charlotte Zolotow. Used by permission of HarperCollins Publishers.

Index

Kurita, Akiko, 8
Kuskin, Karla, 68–81, 216

L

"Ladybird, ladybird, / Fly away home,"
  117, 119–20
Lamb, Charles, 140
Lassie Come Home, 198, 208
Lawson, Robert, 106, 201
Lear, Edward, 92, 124, 125
Lemmons, Bob, 163
Lentil, 106, 108, 109–10, 112, 115
Lester, Julius, 150, 159–60, 161–63
Lewis, Richard, 27
Liddell children, 137–38
Life, 112, 154, 192
Lindbergh, Charles, Jr., 171, 177–78
Liney, John J., 154
Lionni, Leo, 48
Little, Brown, 121
Little Black Sambo, 163–64
Little Elephant, 66–67
Little Engine That Could, The, 32, 83
Little Henry comic strip, 154
Little Match Girl, The, 151
Little Nemo comic strip, 207
Little Red School House, 70–71
Lobel, Arnold, 88–89, 101
Lonely Ones, The, 192–93, 194–95
Long Journeys Home: Stories from Black
  History, 163
Look, 154
Look Again!, 59–60, 65
Look Book, 61
Lord of the Flies, The, 127–28
Lore and Language of Schoolchildren, The,
  127–28, 129
Lorraine, Walter, 89, 98–99
Lowe, David, 201

M

McCarthy, Joseph, 199–200
McCloskey, Robert, 106–16
McDuff books, 205

McKissack, Patricia C., 150
Macmillan, 59–60, 202, 203
Madeline (Bemelmans), 106
Make Way for Ducklings, 106, 107, 110–15,
  116
"Man Who Was a Horse, The," 163
Margaret K. McElderry Books, 142
Marie Antoinette, 83
Marshall, James, 82–105
Marshall, John, 124
Martin, Bill, Jr., 48, 50–51
Martin, Sarah Catherine, 124
Mary on Horseback, 197, 213
Massee, May, 106, 109–10, 112
Math Games, 16
Max and Ruby books, 197, 206–7
Max's Birthday, 206–7
Max's Dragon Shirt, 206–7
Mayer, Mercer, 204
Metropolitan Museum of Art, 49
Millay, Edna St. Vincent, 218
Millet, Jean-François, 11
Milne, A. A., 131
Minty, 159
Mirandy and Brother Wind, 158–59, 160
Misanthrope, The, 104
Miss Nelson books, 82, 95, 99, 102, 103,
  105
Mitchell, Lucy Sprague, 67, 71
Mitsumasa Anno Museum, 8
Mixed-Up Chameleon, The, 55
Molière, 104
Moon, for What Do You Wait?, 27
Moon Was the Best, The, 65, 66
More, Fewer, Less, 59
Morris's Disappearing Bag, 199, 206
Mortimer, Penelope, 127
Mother Goose rhymes, 5, 18, 20, 117,
  120–22, 125–26, 198, 209–10,
  212–13
Mr. Revere and I, 201
Museum of Modern Art, 49, 58, 62
music, 19, 20, 22, 40, 84, 87, 94–95, 108,
  184, 200